KEATS AND CHAPMAN

Tom Mathews

NEW
ISLAND

Keats and Chapman
First published 2008
by New Island
2 Brookside
Dundrum Road
Dublin 14

www.newisland.ie

ISBN 978-1-84840-010-8

All the characters in this book are real and no offence is intended to
anyone imaginary either living or dead.

British Library Cataloguing Data. A CIP catalogue record for this
book is available from the British Library.

Printed in the UK by Athenaeum Press Ltd., Gateshead,
Tyne & Wear

New Island received financial assistance from
The Arts Council (An Chomhairle Ealaíon), Dublin, Ireland.

10 9 8 7 6 5 4 3 2 1

'Tant d'histoire pour quelques calembours.'

Raymond Queneau

My thanks are due to the editors and proprietors
of *In Dublin* magazine and *Hot Press*,
where much of the material in this book
has appeared in slightly different form.

Between what pallid duality of items have I been too busy to commence work on this introduction?

Wan thing and another.

Offa what pedal extremities have I been run?

Me feet.

From the hangover of which progenitor and his helpmeet may I be stated to be making a recovery?

The Mammy and Daddy.

Thereby drawing down from my publisher the abuse of what domestic quadruped whose hair of which I currently stand sorely in want?

Our friend the dog.

What thirty-six-inch intervals were in consequence given out?

Yards.

What sightless particle will this circumstance fail to make?

A blind bit of difference.

When a man like myself is put to the pin of his collar like this, to what, not unattractive, declivity may things be said to have come?

A pretty pass.

Correct. Upon what temporal rowel have I composed the above?

The spur of the moment.

And within the roar of which ungulate will the following adventures be said (in comparison with the originals) not to come?

The ass.

Did Myles know that John Keats really was addicted to puns? In his last surviving letter, Keats wrote to his best friend, 'I have an habitual feeling of my real life having past, and that I am leading a posthumous existence.' Here is prescience indeed: 'Yet I ride the little horse and, at my worst, even in Quarantine, summoned up more puns, in a sort of desperation, in one week, than in any year of my life.' This was written by the poet the week he died. 'I beg leaf to withdraw all my puns – They are all wash and base 'uns'.

'Keats's mind, so alertly prefigurative,' writes Christopher Ricks, 'was especially liable to puns and to portmanteaux, often of course quite premeditatedly: his letters are full of conscious effects of which Lewis Carroll or James Joyce would have been proud.'

Joyce, whose long shadow loomed over Myles (until in exasperation he condemned the master to sewing semmets for the Jesuits in *The Dalkey Archive*) was no slouch himself when it came to wordplay. 'What opera is like a railway line? Rows of cast steel' a proclivity leading inexorably to the Celtic interlace of Finnegans Wake, the apostrophe shunning (because all-inclusive) great book of the night written almost entirely in puns. Multilingual puns at that, creating a language that Michael Frayn has charmingly termed 'Eurish'. Joyce told Frank

Budgen, 'After all, the Holy Roman Catholic Apostolic Church was built on a pun. It ought to be good enough for me.' His last great book draws heavily on the two great dreambooks of Carroll 'We grisly old sykos who did our bit on Alices when they were Jung and easily Freudened.'

To the objection of triviality he replied, 'Yes. Some of the means I use are trivial – and some are quadrivial.' He had sent English to sleep he said but what dreams move in that sleep. *At Swim-Two-Birds* was the last book he was able to read. And he paid Myles the greatest compliment a young man setting out as a writer could receive: 'That's a real writer with the true comic spirit.'

S.J. Perelman was another master of wordplay: Secretary: 'The Dean is furious. He's waxing wroth.' Groucho Marx: 'Oh, is Roth out there too? Tell Roth to wax the Dean for a while.' (Perelman kept a photograph of Joyce on his desk.) Perelman admired Myles hugely, telling Bernard Levin on television in May 1967, 'I have gotten enormous pleasure the last couple of years since the *Irish Times* has been reviving his columns. I think that they are delightful and I've been circulating them around to friends of mine, like Ogden Nash and so forth, and we all agree that this work has tremendous quality.'

Not everyone is a fan of course. Martin Amis, reviewing an anthology of modern humour,

No Laughing Matter (coincidentally the title of Anthony Cronin's 1989 biography of Myles), was saddened to see 'a writer of comic genius represented only by his lugubrious 'Keats and Chapman' concoctions. '"There is a nip in the heir," said Keats, "His B.Arch. is worse than his bight," said Keats.' Puns are cues or triggers to the humourless, and double puns are obviously twice as funny as single ones. Poor Flann! He must have cranked out these duds after lunch, in drunken scorn or cynical despair.'

Perhaps he should have persevered. A man in love with words enough to borrow a 'mineral wind' from Bellow for insertion in a piece of journalism would surely enjoy this frolic that so charmed the late Ben Kiely: (Keats and Chapman are on Vesuvius) 'Watching the bubbling lava and considering the sterile ebullience of the stony entrails of the earth.' The gravitas and horsehair-sofa-prose form the casing of the grenade, the punchline, as long delayed as possible, the pin whose removal causes the explosion at the ear. That extraordinary genius, and I intend no irony, Gilbert Sorrentino dedicated his vast novel *Mulligan Stew* to the memory of Brian O'Nolan, his 'virtue *hilaritas*'. It is a crazy, learned parody of all English literature that owes as much to Myles as it does to Joyce. From this arsenal of received ideas that would have delighted Flaubert,

I extract this sobering Kinbotesque line: 'Keats and Shelley never had any of the conversations that the slanderous Miles O'Nolan attributes to them.'

How were these stories composed? Backwards, from the punchline. After that I say nothing. We kill to dissect. The familiar illustration is the man who has disassembled his watch and put it back together to discover he has one cog left over. Keith Hopper in his *A Portrait of the Artist as a Young Post-Modernist* tells us 'The inner landscape of the Keats-Chapman world is a self-conscious intertextual zone.' 'Your granny, Fergus' one can almost hear Mrs. MacPhellimey interject. As Saul Steinberg has written, 'Trying to define humour is one of the definitions of humour.' You get the best view of Paris from the Eiffel Tower because you can't see the Eiffel Tower from there. And as Ms. Stein, one of that city's more famous alumni has assured us, 'When you get there, there isn't any there there.'

The idea for this book grew out of a conversation the author had with RTÉ's Seamus Hosey at the Myles Symposium held at Newman House in 1986. As I worked intermittently on the manuscript, my constant fear was of unconsciously duplicating one of Myles's originals. If I have done so, my apologies.

I finish this introduction on 1 April, the day of my deadline, coincidentally the day of Myles's

death forty-two years ago. With plenty of 'diffi-
dence of the author' I dedicate on this sad
anniversary, to a man whose own forms of joy I
have so long admired, this musterpass.

Tom Mathews

THE IMPORTANCE OF BEING ERNIE

At the Arts Ball in the Mansion House, Keats was the undisputed hit of the evening as Eric Morecambe. He pretended to catch stones in a paper bag, did impressions of Schnozzle Durante with a Styrofoam cup nose, and put the Lord Mayor in a hammerlock, crying, 'Get out of that!' Inside however, he was seething. Where was Chapman, who was to have impersonated the other half of the famed duo? The hour for judging came and went, but the prize for best team was awarded to Osbert, Sacheverell, and Edith Sitwell as the Three Stooges, with Edith's Curly being singled out for especial commendation. As all filed out into the chilly Kildare Street night in search of taxis, Chapman came panting along on his short fat hairy legs nervously smoothing his hair. 'Sorry I'm late,' he puffed, 'I overslept. I promise it won't happen again.' 'It is easy to be Wise after the event,' snapped Keats.

Usque ad Nauseam

It was not today, (no, nor yesterday) that Keats and Chapman strolled excitedly for the first time about the front square of Trinity College, two "freshers" eager to participate in the fun of the eponymous week. Keats, a strict teetotaller, looked askance at his friend as he signed up to compete in a vulgar display of self-indulgence whereby he was to ingest a large volume of ale from a glass no less than three feet in length without pausing for breath.

To cheers and hallooings from his youthful peers, Chapman achieved the pointless feat despite Keats's condemnatory glances and adjurations to desist from his folly. Moments later Chapman, flushed literally with victory, confessed miserably that he felt like the Spartan youth upon whose vitals the fox had made his repast. 'What am I to do?' he groaned, bent double and clutching at his horribly distended stomach. Keats pounded him vigorously between the shoulder blades. 'Get up the yard,' he admonished.

THE EGGS AND THEY

Keats's poultry business was providing the basis
for a sizeable nest egg when disaster struck. The
local council closed the road to the city, thus
cutting off his lucrative chicken sales. Despite a
prolonged and acrimonious correspondence, the
best suggestion that the faceless bureaucrats could
come up with was that his fleet of trucks make a
circuitous detour, adding sixty miles to a journey
now ruinously expensive given the price of petrol.
These letters – masterpieces of controlled sarcasm
and Swiftian invective – the poet determined to
issue in book form. But what was he to call it?
'How about *The Hen Re-Route Letters*?' suggested
Chapman.

THE HUNGER FOR KNOWLEDGE

By the time Keats and Chapman were enrolled at
Dotheboys Hall, Mr. Squeers's policy of practical
education had extended to mealtimes. Every day
the coarse dumplings that floated in each pupil's
dish of greasy stew were cooked in moulds so as to
resemble various continents, islands, and the
shapes arrived at by the decisions of those who
draw up the internal boundaries of nations. Thus
one hapless child might be ingesting the County
Cork while another chewed listlessly at Lithuania.
One thing, however, was certain: thanks to the extreme smallness of the portions, nobody came
away from the table satisfied except the school's
grasping proprietor. One day Keats, noticing that a
scrap remained in the cooking pot, had the temer-
ity to approach the headmaster holding out his
bowl. 'Please sir,' he quavered, 'I want Samoa.'

BLAME IT ON THE STONES

When Keats was invited to *Those Were the Days My Friend,* an exhibition of paintings of inventors and their inventions by Paul McCartney, he was momentarily torn between *Phonograph Day* (Edison spinning the first disc) and *Model T Day* (Henry Ford in his famous black auto). The picture he selected however was, as Macca explained, inspired by Mick 'n' Keef. This commemorated a Hungarian designer's completion of a cube-shaped puzzle composed of twenty-six parts in six colours fixed to a central spindle, allowing their rotation on three axes. The solved puzzle presented a uniform colour on each face. Keats appeared delighted with the daub. 'Good buy?' enquired Chapman. *'Rubik's cube day,'* said Keats.

PRESERVATION ACT

When Keats's peke Darien passed away after being smothered by George Sand's bottom during a cheese and wine do at the Mansion House, the poet decided to have him stuffed. But as luck would have it, the only taxidermist in the city was booked up for a week stuffing an elephant that had died of a surfeit of buns at the zoo. Remembering the dissecting room and its stench of formaldehyde, Keats determined to acquire some and preserve the little animal in a glass jar. The thing was done, and for many years the jar rested on the piano next to a bust of Beethoven. 'You'd almost think he was alive,' marvelled Chapman one August evening. 'He's with us in spirit,' averred Keats.

Not Always to the Swift

Business was fast and furious at the bookies' tent at the Philosophers reptile race. 'I'm having a hundred to win on Schopenhauer's chameleon,' enthused Chapman, 'How about you, old man?' Keats looked cunning and, touching his nose in a significant manner, remarked, 'Of what we know not, thereof we cannot speak.' 'Did you hear something?' demanded Chapman eagerly. 'Put your shirt on Wittgenstein's track tortoise,' advised the poet.

A TAXING SITUATION

Keats had the owner of a number of retail outlets on the carpet. As a special investigator for the Revenue Commissioners, he was a whale on would-be tax evaders. 'I accept your returns on Scents, the perfume business, and Sounds, the music shop, but what of the figures for your restaurant? Failure to produce them could result in not alone a fine, but a term of imprisonment. Chapman (for it was he whom Keats was thus pursuing with the added bitterness of an old friend) sneered defiantly. 'Do your worst,' he challenged, 'I can do the time standing on my head.' 'There's no accounting for *Tastes*,' said Keats.

Travelling Hopefully

When Keats and Chapman were hired as designers by Iarnród Éireann, Chapman's posters won many international awards, and he swiftly rose to become head of the art department. Keats, alas, proved so feeble a performer that he was entrusted only with the most menial of tasks. To Chapman fell the distasteful business of rejecting most of his loyal but ham-fisted colleague's productions. After Keats had submitted a particularly awful specimen, he badgered the unfortunate Chapman for days and finally demanded, 'What did you really think of my day return ticket?' 'I'll get back to you on it,' said Chapman evasively.

AN IMPROBABLE MEAL

On a flight over the Andes, Keats and Chapman were bored brainless by an overly voluble octogenarian. Suddenly, a lightning bolt took off the left wing and the plane went down in the desolate snow. Our heroes were the only survivors. After days of hunger, they resorted to cannibalism. Keats made a fire of twigs and bits of the wreckage and was soon gnawing the elbow of the oldster who had so bored them earlier. An hour later he was pale and trembling. 'What's the matter, old fellow?' enquired Chapman, munching contentedly on a rib. 'My heart aches and a drowsy numbness pains my sense as though of hemlock I had drunk,' replied the poet. But, brightening, he continued, 'I expect it's just some dull O.A.P. I ate.' Chapman was violently ill.

NOTHING TO BE DONE

Among the select few invited to attend the premiere of Samuel Beckett's *Breath* were his old friends Keats and Chapman (known affectionately to the author as Gogo and Didi). Somewhere in the Marais at a locale unknown to the paparazzi, an old clochard gasped his last on a tiny stage. After fifty protracted wheezes he was gone. Dim, then faintly glimmering, the light faded. Alas, when the house lights came on it was all too obvious that the distinguished first night audience, with the exception of our heroes, had availed of the friendly darkness to make good their escape.

Beckett's eyes glinted behind bottle-thick lenses. 'Where did I go wrong?' he murmured, his voice like autumn leaves moved over dry grass by a chill wind. 'Sam,' said Keats, 'you made the pants too long.'

Pardon His Glove

When Keats laid out a cur who had impugned May Oblong's character, a Garda who had observed the altercation remarked, 'You're pretty handy with the mitts.' Over a brace of stouts, he convinced the hero that with the right tuition (he had himself won the Garda silver medal, Heavyweight Champion 1932), he stood a fair chance of earning a golden fortune in the ring. After a period of intensive training, a money fight was arranged between the young hopeful and Jack Doyle (The Gorgeous Gael). All Dublin was in attendance at the national stadium for the sport. After Doyle had sung the national anthem and Keats had recited *Endymion*, the Archbishop of Dublin blessed the gloves and the Lord Mayor, Alfie Byrne, jumped into the ring to referee and see fair play.

Alas, at an early stage in the proceedings, Keats, momentarily distracted by a press photographer's flashbulb, took a tremendous clout to the jaw and was counted out. It was all over bar the shouting of which you may be assured there was no shortage from the disappointed throng. The trainer was inconsolable and departed to drown his sorrows. It was left to the faithful Chapman to sponge reviving iced water on his poor friend's brow. 'What happened?' croaked Keats, coming round. 'You let down your guard,' said Chapman.

IT SLIPPED HIS MIND

As he grew older, Chapman's memory steadily dis-improved. One day he remarked, 'Y'know Keats, I'm encountering the most tremendous difficulty in distinguishing between the austere disciple of Zeno and Sakyamuni or Gautama, founder of that religious system of spiritual purity.' 'You can't tell stoic from Buddha,' said Keats. But perhaps all this is better forgotten.

There were not a few who ascribed the unprecedentedly rapid rise of Keats through the labyrinthine complexities of the Church of Rome to the machinations and backstairs dealings of his wily aide, Cardinal Chapman. In fact, his meteoric rise detailed in the Chapman-ghosted 'autobiography' (*From P.P. to Pontiff in just two weeks*) was widely considered the inspiration for the late Baron Corvo's *Hadrian VII*.

Be that as it may, certain of the Curia were of the opinion that the celerity of his elevation had contributed in no small measure to the new pope's increasingly obvious eccentricity: his habits of breaking into old George Formby numbers while accompanying himself on the banjulele during *Urbi et Orbi* and dressing as Spongebob Squarepants while washing the feet of the poor occasioned particular disquiet among the more conservative.

Even Chapman became somewhat uneasy when the Angelic Shepherd announced his intention of ending the global warming crisis by miraculously lowering the level of the world's oceans. 'Should I shrink the sea?' he enquired. 'I reckon you should see the shrink,' advised Chapman.

From Those Wonderful Folks Who Gave You Hiroshima

'You see,' explained the Art Executive to the Art Director (Keats) and Copy Chief (Chapman), 'what the client wants here is an image that makes eating his junk food seem "cool". I wish you gentlemen the very best of luck.' So saying he left the boardroom for a protracted liquid lunch.

Shortly thereafter, Keats produced a visual featuring a group of prosperous-looking citizens (movie stars, rocking boys, captains of industry, etc.), tucking into the client's burgers and onion rings with every indication of relish. 'Not bad,' allowed Chapman, regarding it critically. 'Yet something's missing.' He pointed to a space in the ethnically correct composition beside an Arab chieftain gobbling a spicefurter with fries. 'How about a Burgher to go with that Sheikh?' he suggested.

THE COLLECTOR

When Keats was at Oxford, he became an inveterate collector of trivia. His rooms were stuffed with curios. Netsuke, ships in bottles, fans, coprolites, a set of the works of John D. Sheridan bound in human skin, and similar outré items lay piled any which way without apparent system. On holiday alone in Egypt, Keats fell in with an amusing old Irishman who, for the price of a few beers, sold him a human ear, the sole grisly remnant of an English officer he had despatched to kingdom come in a dynamiting operation in the County Kerry back in '21. News of this acquisition reached Chapman via a mutual friend who had bumped into Keats at the old bazaar in Cairo. When, bronzed and fit, the poet arrived back a few weeks later, he displayed his new prize on the mantelpiece. When Chapman called round to tea, the noisome relic caught his eye at once. 'I see you got a bit of a Tan while you were away,' he observed. Keats sighed wearily.

Take Me Out To The Ball Game

When Keats's friend Ed de Maggio took up baseball, Keats invariably struck out against him. His feats on the pitcher's mound were legendary, so it was with infinite regret that Chapman brought the sad news to the poet that de Maggio had become incurably insane and had been confined to a little rubber room in a high-class loony bin in Washington.

They decided to visit the hapless athlete to see if they could do anything to alleviate his distress. They found him physically well but grown enormously fat, for his madness consisted in subsisting on a diet of hot dogs and salted dry-roasted peanuts to the exclusion of all other foodstuffs. He suggested that his friends join him in this repast. Nothing loath they readily acquiesced, but after many nuts and a brace of mustard-slathered franks, they called for a draught of cool water. Ed said that the water from the asylum's well was far better than tap water and that he'd return with a jug of same in a trice. An hour passed. Then another, by which time the pair were expiring with thirst. At last he returned with the healing draught and explained that he had lost his bearings and wandered many miles out of his way. 'It's the cracked pitcher that goes longest to the well,' said Keats.

THE ITALIAN JOB

When Keats and Chapman were down on their luck in Como, they got work as kitchen porters in a local restaurant. Two of the waiters, a pair of hot-blooded cousins from Napoli, were forever bickering. One evening they came to blows when Enrico, the larger of the two, sneered openly at Luigi's rendition of one of Emily Dickinson's poems. The manager watched aghast as spaghetti and rough red wine spattered the indignant diners.

To cool their ardour, the quick-thinking Keats seized a dish of eels from the icebox and dropped them one at a time on the antagonists. 'Yoora friend,' the manager said to Chapman, 'why he do theesa thing?' 'He's piling eels on troubled waiters,' Chapman explained.

CULTURAL LEANINGS

Looking smart in their uniforms, Keats and Chapman efficiently herded a bunch of eager tourists aboard the bus to Pisa. Employed as tour guides by Turin Tours (our motto 'Keep on Tourin'') they set off on their whistle-stop journey: 'Five cities in five days: Rome, Pisa, Venice, Milan, and (thanks to a printer's error) Miami'. As the clapped-out bus limped along the dusty roads, our heroes made the welcome suggestion that their group break for "refreshment" at a picturesque wine bar, just ten miles from their second destination. Alas, all drank not wisely but overwell of a local vintage that rapidly induced in the imbiber the impression that everything was leaning (the natives used this particular beverage for dissolving axle grease). After sleeping for hours on the coach, everyone awoke hot and sticky and leaning on each other, out the windows, or on what fragments of sanity remained. Arriving at their destination the next day, Keats and Chapman formed the group into two straggling lines. 'Wait here for ten minutes and we'll arrange a trip to the fabled leaning tower,' assured Keats. Chapman and himself hurried off for a cure but so enjoyed the first that it led to another, and when they staggered from their shady seats back to their charges, it was to discover that they had disappeared.

'That's it then,' groaned Keats, 'we'll be fired for sure now.' 'We should've minded our Pisan queues,' admitted Chapman.

Uneasy Money

'How sharper than a serpent's tooth it is to have a thankless child,' quoted Keats elegantly, as Chapman ranted on about his eldest boy's extravagances and want of appreciation. 'The amount I expend on his education at one of the better public schools alone is practically astronomical, as I have to constantly remind him. But does he listen? It's all water off a duck's back.' He heaved a great sigh. 'Eton bread is soon forgotten,' allowed Keats.

When Keats joined the Pre-Raphaelites, Chapman, whose talent lay more in the area of letters than the sister art of painting, went to study criticism under Ruskin. Keats struck up a friendship with Holman Hunt and left with him for the Holy Land. Hunt started work on his famous *Scapegoat* (utilising the coarse grain of Keats's beard as inspiration), but after a series of discussions, Keats decided that their views of Bible interpretation differed too widely and left for the fabled resting place of the Ark.

Here he painted for a year. But the tiresome eye for detail of his brothers in the movement was a hampering influence on the Byzantine excess of his romantic vision, so after limning the mountain's outline at lightning speed, he filled the foreground with a spirited rendition of Noah's daughters frolicking in a state of nature, in a style combining the solidity of Rubens with the frivolous lubricity of Boucher.

A year later, Keats's masterpiece hung alongside the better-known works of the Brotherhood. Ruskin and Chapman were, of course, present at the opening. The prudish Chapman was as appalled as his mentor at Keats's offering and roundly condemned this latest manifestation of "the fleshy school of Painting". 'And what is worse, the deplorable want of that meticulous fidelity to nature that has hitherto been the hallmark of the group,' tutted Ruskin. Keats was unmoved by their censures and remarked cheerfully, 'I don't know much about Ararat but I know what I like.'

An Oeuf is an Oeuf

Thanks to an unusually shrewd investment on the horses, Keats and Chapman found themselves enabled to spend a month in the South of France. Here, through an acquaintance of Keats's, a Miss Hill (it was the irrepressible Chapman's wont to refer to her as a grand colline altogether), they were introduced to an estate agent of extraordinary stupidity. Our heroes made it known that they wished to rent one of his maisons in the Boulevard St Michel. Hours of haggling ensued, but no agreement was reached. Keats flew into a rage, and to emphasise a point, he brought his fist crashing down on a box of eggs the recalcitrant businessman had purchased earlier for his petit déjeuner. Cowed by this action, the fellow speedily furnished a month's lease to which our heroes as speedily signed their names.

A week or so after moving in, Chapman remonstrated with his friend as follows: 'Look here mon vieux. It's all very well making a point, but I feel we could have done without your show of temper. Noblesse oblige and all that. Our duty to set these chaps an example.' Keats lit a Gauloise and, exhaling a blue plume, remarked, 'Au contraire. You can't make un homme let without breaking eggs.'

THE ROAR OF THE GREASEPAINT, THE SMELL OF THE CROWD

It has been remarked with no little justification that there were those among the Surrealists, that colourful band, whom it would be charitable to call eccentric. So it was that when Antonin Artaud paid a fleeting visit to these shores, his antic disposition proved too rich for the thin blood of theatrical Dublin. The Abbey rejected out of hand his suggestion of a production of *Marat/Sade* and his portrayal of the late John Charles McQuaid as a cannibal necrophile was universally adjudged the one weak spot in Jack Cruise's *Holiday Hayride* at the Theatre Royal. Embittered and estranged, he roamed the house in which Keats and Chapman, staunch supporters of the avant garde, were putting him up and indeed (for the flesh is weak) just about putting up with him. A man whose idea of a good time is to howl like a rabid pig through the night is a difficult companion.

The pair were delighted therefore when their guest announced that he had at last found some enlightened artists who appreciated him for what he was and who had offered him both accommodation and a chance to mount a production at their theatre, an oasis of culture in the sea of Philistia that constituted the Dublin of the time. 'Despite his utter insanity he certainly seems to have charmed Hilton and Michael,' observed Chapman. 'He's a way with the fairies,' agreed Keats.

THE FOLDING GREEN

When Keats was appointed Minister for Finance, one of his first actions was to call for the submission of new designs for the nation's currency. Chapman was first to appear, excitedly waving his sketchbook. 'Here's my proposal,' he cried. 'It's a freshly-mowed lawn,' he elucidated. 'With its connotations of decency and order it suggests reliability. And green (our national colour, need I add?) has long been associated in the popular mind with banknotes.' 'That's the maddest suggestion I've ever heard,' said Keats wearily. 'It's the maddest thing since Mad Jack McMad won the Maddest Man in Madland Contest.' (Keats's favourite television programme was *Blackadder*.) 'You're a plain-spoken man,' said Chapman admiringly. 'I don't mint swards,' said Keats.

A PAINFUL CASE

Keats's impressions of cartoon characters were a constant source of annoyance to the fastidious Chapman. 'Don't have a cow man,' Keats would counsel his old friend, causing the worthy fellow endless irritation. So it was with some relief that Chapman learned that Keats had got a job with a local pharmaceutical laboratory, and swept off with a valedictory, 'Yabba dabba doo.'

It was soon evident to Keats's supervisor that his newest recruit's aesthetic sense extended from poesy into the sister art of the visual. For in a short time Keats had designed an aspirin so attractive that it outsold all other commercial brands. In awarding Keats a handsome bonus for his efforts, his employer remarked, 'Mr. Keats, I attribute our top notch sales of this product to the wonderfully fashionable appearance of the capsule you've designed.' 'Yes,' allowed Keats, 'it's smarter than the average Bayer.' Everyone in the room immediately took several.

A SOUND MAN

As it had been Chapman's boyhood dream to gain employment in Radio Éireann, one can only imagine his sensations on being informed, as a man in his thirties, of his success in securing the position of trainee sound effects man in the drama department. His first assignment was a detective mystery. As the tale unravelled, his footsteps were to be recorded as those of a sinister malefactor. The week after his debut, he and Keats bent over the wireless listening eagerly. Sure enough, the footfalls combined with a judiciously chosen musical accompaniment evoked a suitably eerie atmosphere. 'Congratulations my dear fellow,' said Keats. 'You must be delighted at this achievement.' 'I'm walking on air,' said Chapman.

Chapman was in a severe state of the jigs and had partaken of no solids in days. Anxious for his old friend's wellbeing, the soft-hearted Keats prevailed on a friend, the owner of a successful art gallery, to hire his errant sidekick as general caretaker of his establishment and its contents. 'The thing is,' he explained to the trembling and unshaven Chapman, 'that you'll have all the wine you can drink and snacks you can eat at the weekly openings.' A couple of weeks later Keats was pleased to encounter his friend clean-shaven, well-dressed and prosperous-looking. 'The position has proved satisfactory then?' he enquired. 'There's curatin' and cure drinkin' in it,' said Chapman.

SOMEWHAT OFF-THE-WALL

Exhausted by lifting heavy sea chests and the effort that hurling them into the waves entailed, Keats and Chapman took a welcome break from the Boston Tea Party to sit on a wall. 'This puts me in mind of the nursery rhyme,' said Keats. 'Which one?' enquired Chapman. 'Hump tea, dump tea,' replied the poet. Ignoring this, his resilient associate passed the remark that it was a poor summer and that heavy rains were predicted. 'Never mind,' said Keats, 'we'll probably have a great Fall.' Chapman descended into a moody silence.

WHERE THERE'S A WILL

When Chapman's rich uncle passed on, himself and Keats attended the reading of the will with much interest, for as usual they found themselves in strait-ened circumstances. Judge therefore of their cha-grin when it was discovered to the pair that his sole legacy to Chapman was a cheap alarm clock along with a note to the effect that it might serve to 'Wake up his ideas and get all that poetic nonsense out of his head.' Later, Keats noticed him moodily turning the little key at the small timepiece's back. 'What are you doing?' he enquired listlessly. 'I'm winding up his estate,' Chapman explained.

THE END OF AN ERA

At a press screening of *The Shootist*, Keats and Chapman reminisced sadly on a golden age now gone, lamenting, as men will, the passing of the good old 'shoot 'em up' Western adventure film. '*Stagecoach*,' said Chapman, '*Gunfight at the O.K. Corral, High Noon*. They don't make 'em like that anymore.' 'We're watching a genre wane,' agreed Keats.

WHERE NO WATERS ARE

Fog swirled about the little airport and hung thickly in the leaves of the swaying palms as Keats and Chapman turned up the collars of their trench-coats and strained in the tropic night to catch the drone of an incoming plane. Their exit visas had been validated, so it was with some surprise that they saw the cheerful little French police chief of Casablanca exit his car and, saluting, hand Keats a letter.

Keats tore open the envelope. It was from the editor of a top literary weekly. 'Dear John – I return your manuscript on the mathematical diversions Carroll invented for the amusement of Alice and her sisters. It lacks, I think, sufficient popular appeal. Besides, I received in the afternoon post a fascinating account from our mutual friend of how a head cold led to the composition of a memoir he has entitled *Borstal Boy*. I reckon it's a cracker. Yours in an agony of haste.'

'What a let-down,' sighed Keats, having read this disheartening screed to his colleague. 'In this crazy world,' said Chapman, 'the problems of three Liddell people don't amount to an ill of Behan's,' knowing even as he uttered the words that he would live to regret them, maybe not now or tomorrow, but soon and for the rest of his life.

Through the turbid darkness came the throb of a light aircraft, or was it just the vein in his poor temple, Keats wondered.

THERE'S GOLD IN THEM THAR ILLS

After much painstaking research, Keats succeeded in discovering what had eluded science since time immemorial: a cure for the common cold. Within minutes of ingesting a simple azure spansule, the miseries of sore throat, blocked nose and fever completely vanished. The sole drawback of the medication was that the patient gained up to five stone in the days following his or her recovery. However, this was a temporary inconvenience and in every case the excess weight disappeared in a week or two.

'You must be making a pretty penny,' remarked Chapman as he helped his friend carry a large canvas bag of banknotes to his safe. 'I've swelled the coughers considerably,' allowed Keats.

ON THE GRAND CANAL

En route to the pub a rich uncle had willed to Keats, our heroes encountered a beggar selling aromatic reeds on the canal bank. In a position to dispense largesse for once, Keats gave the fellow a tenner and strolled along cutting at the weeds in the grass verges with his acquisition. When one of the customers, a botanist, expressed interest in the growth, Keats was happy to surrender it. Later in the evening however, the fellow became intoxicated and abusive and was the cause of so much trouble that Chapman was forced to physically eject him. 'I thought I handled that rather well for a beginner,' he said, dusting his hands. 'You gave him the bum's rush,' said Keats.

The Fly in the Ointment

Our heroes were once again facing ruin. Their patent embrocation had been analysed by the Food Safety Authority and found wanting. In fact, in a closely written 500-page official document, it had been adjudged entirely inefficacious if not actually dangerously toxic. 'Alas,' groaned Keats, 'all our dreams are come to naught and public humiliation and certain bankruptcy are sure to be our portion thanks to this accursed product.' He squirted a little of the valueless solution onto a palm. 'And we have no one to blame but ourselves.' He glared angrily at the gelid droplet. 'Don't rub it in,' sighed Chapman.

THE WAGES OF SIN

Inspector Keats chuckled as he slipped the hand-cuffs onto the wrists of shivering cat burglar Chapman. The long manhunt had ended when Chapman, surprised during a dawn swoop, wearing only a pair of shorts, was pursued until cornered in the ice-room of a nearby abattoir. 'So it ends like this,' said Keats, 'You see where your folly has led you.' 'You've got me cold,' admitted Chapman.

The first indication that Chapman was losing his mind was when he wasted three hours trying to explain the plot of *Goldilocks and the Three Bears* to Marty Whelan. Soon the men in the white coats arrived with a large net, and in no time he was incarcerated in the locked ward in St. Pat's.

When Keats visited him with grapes and Lucozade, the patient gave no sign of recognition, addressing all his remarks instead to a small stuffed bird which stood on his bedside table. 'Yes,' he said, 'I have taken my medication. You suggest that I take a nap? Very well, you know best.' With this cryptic utterance he fell at once into a profound slumber.

'How is your poor friend getting on?' enquired an acquaintance of the poet the next day. 'I'm afraid he's taken a tern for the nurse,' replied Keats.

All to Play For

When Tom Petty broke up The Heartbreakers to captain Sligo Rovers, he led his team to victory after victory. Twenty counties fell before them. All was to play for as just one match remained between Tom's implacable squad and the purple robe of triumph. 'Sligo for the cup,' was everywhere the cry. In the bookie's, Chapman counselled Keats to put his chemise on the underdog. The poet seemed lost in thought. 'No,' he said pensively, 'I won't back Down.'

Alarmed by his increasingly obvious alcoholism and irrational obsession with horoscopes, Keats had Chapman committed to a drying-out clinic. Visiting him one New Year's Eve, Keats waited vainly whilst an obliging orderly went in search of his friend. At last he was located in the room of nonagenarian soak Rabbie Laing, grandfather of the more famous R.D., iconoclastic author of 1970s bestseller *Knots*. 'Sorry old fellow,' blurted Chapman when he at last arrived, 'completely slipped my mind that you were coming. Rabbie's a Sagittarius you see, and we were having a frightfully interesting conversation.' 'Should old acquaintance be forgot,' asked Keats patiently, 'for the sake of Auld Laing's sign?'

TO EACH HIS OWN

One balmy summer night as they strolled along Sackville Street after a few drinks in the Green Room of the Gate Theatre, Keats and Chapman fell to discussing the slightly unorthodox relationship between their hosts Hilton and Michael. 'Church and State alike frown on this sort of thing,' observed Chapman. A tram bell punctuated their discourse. 'Yet,' he continued, heedless of the interruption, 'they appear to delight in flouting the conventions.' Keats thought a moment. 'They're happy out,' he said.

A Good Man is Hard to Find

When Keats became sheriff of Deadwood, he and his faithful deputy Chapman vowed to bring law and order to that desolate locale. He soon devised an ingenious method of anticipating the stratagems of evildoers by eavesdropping on the plans of renegade Indians or hired gunmen alike – in the guise of a giant cactus.

From time to time of course, a spine worked its way inside his costume, occasioning him no little distress. The desert heat proved a gruelling test of his endurance. 'Isn't your camouflage awfully uncomfortable?' enquired Chapman solicitously one sweltering morning as Keats prepared to blend seamlessly into the landscape. 'It goes with the territory,' said Keats.

Before the Pen had Gleaned

When Keats and Chapman lived in Paris they became great friends of the eponymous Watt. He introduced them to Mr. Knott, who became an intimate of Keats's. Soon they were well nigh inseparable, and the poet came to rely on his new comrade's erudition, incorporating many of his aperçus into the body of his work. Alas, a dispute arose between the chums. Its cause? Reader, it was a woman. Keats, a veritable dartboard when it came to Cupid's amorous projectiles, fell like a ton of coals for a pretty but featherheaded waitress at Maxim's. Knott spoke slightingly of her intelligence after she had asserted that giraffes reproduce by laying eggs, and the besotted Keats challenged him to a duel. By an astonishing fluke, Keats shot his opponent clean through the heart the following dawn at Versailles.

Remorse set in a few days later. 'If only I hadn't been so foolishly hot-headed,' he lamented to Chapman as he searched vainly for an elusive reference, 'the poor fellow would have found the passage I seek in a trice.' 'Waste Knott, want Knott,' retorted Chapman.

A CHRISTMAS MYSTERY

Things were tough at Christmas for Keats and Chapman. So much so that they resorted to dressing as elves and working as Santa's assistants in Clerys. Long hours they toiled, packing Kens and Barbies in pink paper and cap guns and toy whistles in blue. Beads of sweat formed on the plastic icebergs and ran down the noble brows of our heroes, who grew daily fonder of King Herod. At last the job was finished and they staggered out into the foggiest Christmas Eve in memory. 'Gosh,' remarked Keats, whose poetic soul had never relinquished its belief in that other Claus residence at the North Pole, 'I wonder how the real Santa will find his way tonight?' 'The deer nose,' said Chapman testily.

Chapman had the local bar driven mad with his obsessive talk of Homer. 'The many-minded is going to make me lose mine,' as one (unusually literate) punter put it to Keats one evening. 'Can't you do something about it?'

So it was that Keats got Chapman a job as usher at the nearby cinema, and peace temporarily reigned. But soon things were worse than ever. All his talk now was of the poor conditions at work, and his tedious impressions of Bogart and John Wayne rendered his company less desirable than ever. 'Fat lot of good that's done,' complained an acquaintance to Keats a week or two later, 'it hasn't improved him worth a darn.' 'It's no cine cure,' agreed Keats.

THE SWEET TONGUE OF THE GAEL

From the white sky a whiter sun roasted the rocks and heather. Flies buzzed, but the birds were too weary to sing. Brushing aside a cloud of midges, Keats and Chapman flung off their clothes and plunged into the cooling stream that meandered through the part of the Kerry Gaeltacht where they were staying to renew their acquaintance with the first language. After floating contentedly on their backs for a time, our heroes emerged to find that half their clothes had gone missing and were now doubtlessly adorning some lucky knight of the road. Cursing their misfortune, each broke into a eulogy of his garment. Never was a pair of britches to equal the luscious corduroy articles of Chapman seen west of the Shannon. 'And where,' enquired Keats rhetorically, 'in a day's journey would you find the like of his tweed jacket for resisting thorn and tempest?' At last, they draped themselves with leaves, lamenting as with one voice, 'Ní beidh ar leath éadaí arís ann,' and strode out into the bright day.

REMEMBRANCE OF THINGS PAST

After a fulfilling career as a representative of Guinness breweries, Chapman at length retired to the sleepy medieval paradise of Kilkenny. When his old pal Keats called by, they strolled the quaint streets cutting up the old touches and recollecting the quondam days of their nonage. Eventually they fetched up at the door of Sheehy's bar, one of the premises that in years gone by had been regularly supplied with porter by the hard working Chapman. They determined to enter for some light refreshment. The barman, himself an old man, reminisced with them about the original owner, now long gone to his eternal reward. 'Aye,' said Chapman, 'many's the keg of stout I sold him.' 'And did you once sell Sheehy plain?' enquired the minion. Keats sighed deeply.

GET A WEIGH OUT OF THAT

When Keats and Chapman opened their toyshop, Keats sat up all night making a tiny clown's outfit for the scales they kept on the counter for weighing out marbles, which they sold, like bull's-eyes, by the pound. Then there was such inflating of balloons, bending of bunnies into humorous shapes, Meccano assembly, and like activity as to render the establishment a fair simulacrum of Santa's workshop at the North Pole. Alas, when they opened for business, not a single customer made an appearance. By three in the afternoon, Chapman flew into a rage and, seeking something on which to vent his passion, seized the clown's outfit and tore it to shreds.

The next day business took off, and they discovered that they had opened on a bank holiday. Chapman, abashed at his previous bad behaviour, sat up all night in his turn recreating his partner's handiwork. When Keats entered the shop, the scales were resplendent as before. 'You see,' Chapman said, 'I've atoned for my bad behaviour.' 'You've redressed the balance,' allowed Keats.

A Close Run Thing

Not one for doing things by halves, Keats trained hard for the Dublin marathon, knocking off the jar and cutting out the cigarettes entirely. He assured Chapman that he was determined to win the race. Came the day at last and Keats, well in front with only a mile in it, looked certain to succeed. Then out of nowhere came a surprise challenge from a swarthy but skeletal Latvian, hundreds of whose countrymen roared their support while denigrating the luckless Keats and, in some instances, pelting him with sandwiches, soft drink bottles, crisp packets, and other garbage. Despite the barrage of trash and abuse, he breasted the tape a full three yards ahead of his dusky rival. The good-humoured Irish spectators gave him a well earned ovation. 'Phew,' he exclaimed to Chapman, 'that was hard going.' 'You ran the gaunt Lett,' agreed Chapman.

To Chapman's astonishment, Keats invented a machine that rendered music more absolute. For example, it made B sharp sharper and C minor smaller still. 'This is all well and good my dear fellow,' Chapman allowed, 'but I think you'll have your work cut out for you with E flat.' Truer words were never spoken, for try as he might and despite the great commercial success of his other modifications, he could find no takers for this particular key. 'It's as I said,' chuckled Chapman, 'flatter E will get you nowhere.'

ROUND AND ROUND

Keats determined to write a screenplay about the existential dilemma, the absurdity of life in a post-Death-of-God universe. 'It will be about a man condemned to live the same day again and again,' he explained to Chapman. 'One feature of the grinding monotony will be the diet to which the protagonist is subjected. For breakfast, dinner, and tea he gets only a tasteless hash of coarse pork mince.' 'What d'you propose to call this gleeless analysis of the quotidian?' enquired the ever patient Chapman. '*Ground Hog Day*,' chuckled Keats.

MONEY

Keats and Chapman were strolling aimlessly about the city one beautiful morning discussing their want of ambition and contrasting their situation with that of an old schoolfellow whose industry and Gatsby-like determination to improve himself had made him a millionaire before he was twenty. By one of those extraordinary coincidences that keep happening, it was at this very moment that the individual so recently adverted to was borne past in an immaculate Rolls Royce Silver Shadow, whose elegant chauffeur drew attention to the circumstance by sounding the horn. They had just enough time to glimpse their old acquaintance as he sped by, barking instructions to his broker into a mobile held in his right hand while manipulating an electric shaver with his left. 'He never lets up for a minute,' marvelled Chapman. 'He's a driven man,' allowed Keats.

MOTHER KNEW BEST

Keats, a gifted saxophonist fallen on hard times, was reduced to giving lessons on the instrument at five shillings an hour. His tiny apartment rang to torturous versions of 'Danny Boy', 'Greensleeves', and 'The Rose of Tralee'. His clients were the usual assemblage of anonymities and hopeless dreamers, and Chapman visited his old friend but infrequently as he found these grey non-entities inexpressibly drab and depressing. Judge therefore of his astonishment when one afternoon, on the way up the stairs, he brushed past the imposing figure of Speranza coming down. 'My dear fellow,' he exclaimed, 'surely Lady Wilde has not applied to you for lessons.' 'Why no,' smiled Keats, 'it was on behalf of her son Oscar that she was making an application. He is a brilliant boy and she is convinced he will make his mark in the Arts.' 'But this is splendid,' said Chapman, 'Such a pupil will provide a welcome contrast to the vermin you have hitherto instructed.' 'One should always have someone sensational to train in the reed,' agreed Keats.

WORDS AT WILL

One pupil in Keats's *Expand Your Vocabulary* class had attained the overripe old age of 100. This centenarian's dilemma was that he was incapable of furnishing a synonym for any adjective, however simple. It was Chapman who suggested that this oldster be supplied with a list of words to memorise, which he himself set about devising. The next day, he provided Keats with the following felicitous selection: cheery, blithe, genial, sunny, carefree, bright, debonair, sparkling, breezy, and light-hearted. Within a week, the venerable scholar had memorised the lesson. 'Congratulations,' enthused Keats to his modest assistant, 'you've made an old man vary "happy".'

Back on the Road Again

The one eccentricity that distinguished Keats as a top Hollywood agent was his chosen mode of transportation, a clown's "Krazy Kar" he had purchased on a whim when a circus closed down. He had had this insane-looking vehicle customised with a Rolls Royce engine and, as a crowning touch of ludicrousness, had insisted on welding the familiar RR corporate logo to the hood. One day on the way from Alan Alda's house to that of irascible Italian director Bernardo Bertolucci, Chapman once again pointed out the incongruity, not to say eccentricity, of a man of Keats's position driving a car with doors of different colours, a cuckoo for a horn and a radiator that constantly emitted a series of jets of rainbow-coloured steam. As they shuddered to a halt and a sign reading "Seven days in this make one weak" fell into the gutter accompanied by both fenders, Keats remarked, 'It gets me from A.A. to B.B.'

THE SEASON TO BE JOLLY

That frigid phenomenon the snow was up to its traditional ineluctable antics, falling on the central plain, the dark mutinous Shannon waves and the threshing billows of the turbulent Atlantic. Yes, the newspapers were right: snow was general all over Ireland. Its dark and silver flakes fluttered too on the dizzy heads of Keats and Chapman who, God shrive them, had partaken freely of wine, beer, absinthe – the glaucous temptress – mulled port thick with Gibraltar oranges, and uncountable pints of fine stout. They staggered through the capital, now tripping over a sleeping beggar, now pausing, the better to appreciate a neon simulacrum of jovial St. Nicholas and his reindeer heavily encumbered with every variety of flummery and gewgaw. Realising suddenly that they had eaten nothing since the day before, Chapman suggested that they cook the turkey over a chestnut seller's hissing brazier, but the bird had been mislaid hours before in an early opener. What to do? Then into Keats's consciousness (or what remained of that delicate construct) swam the flashing announcement "King Wenceslas' Pizza Palace". In a trice our heroes were seated with a waiter wearing a cardboard crown in attendance. 'How would you like your pizza, gentlemen?' he enquired unctuously. Keats sat a moment in thought. 'Deep pan, crisp and even,' he ordered.

FOOD FOR THOUGHT

Many of the great and good were present at the Gourmet Food Fair in the Mansion House. Alas none of that throng displayed any interest (whatsoever) in Chapman's stall, which consisted in its entirety of a small assortment of odoriferous goat's cheese. 'D'you think I'll manage to shift any?' he asked Keats disconsolately. Keats brightened (visibly) as David Beckham's lovely wife drew near, looking every inch as if she knew what she wanted, what she really, really wanted. 'If Posh comes to chèvre...' said Keats.

YOU CAN'T GET THE WOOD

Chapman's pulchritudinous niece, Assumpta, had been cast as Tennessee Williams' angst-ridden and fragile heroine in the Abbey's production of *A Streetcar Named Desire*. Keats was despatched by Bertie Smyllie to review it for *The Irish Times*. Unfortunately, her broad Cavan accent rendered the pathos of the playwright's words ludicrous in the extreme, causing the sophisticates in the first night audience to rock with uncontrollable laughter. 'How was her performance?' Chapman enquired the next day, after the curtain had fallen for the first and last time on the hapless waif. 'She Blanched risibly,' said Keats.

A WEIGHTY MATTER

Middle age having brought fame and affluence to Keats and Chapman, they determined to holiday in the United States. Scanning a copy of *What's On in New York City?* as they dined at Elaine's, they were pleased to see that their old friends the Rolling Stones were playing that night. They sank back into their expensive seats at the concert that evening, marvelling at how his arduous lifestyle had preserved Keith's youthful figure while their own had gone the way of all sedentary flesh. The crowd waited with growing impatience for the world's most elegantly wasted axeman to start proceedings and began grumbling as he tried pocket after pocket clearly in want of some essential item. 'He hasn't a pick on him,' said Keats.

FROM THE GAELIC

Keats and Chapman sat starving in a little stone cabin in the Kerry Gaeltacht. Their appetites for beauty they could at any rate assuage and to this end were listening to a gramophone rendition of the lovely 'Das Wohltemperirte Klavier', a plaster bust of whose composer their dog was chewing listlessly in lieu of a bone. 'Is uafásach an ocras atá orm,' groaned Chapman, rubbing his grumbling stomach through his threadbare chemise. Keats shrugging indicated the animal in the corner. 'Gnaw Bach leis,' he suggested.

BREAD ON THE WATERS

One Christmas, Keats hit on a clever scheme. By cross-breeding parrots with homing pigeons, he developed a bird of exotic plumage with both an attractive gift for mimicry and a strong homing instinct. His plan was to sell the birds to pet shops, from which they would take the first opportunity to make good their escape and return to him for resale. By this stratagem of infinite recycling, he hoped to realise a considerable profit on his original investment. 'How is the business working out?' Chapman enquired when a couple of weeks had elapsed. 'I trust you have been successful?' 'They're flying out of the shops,' said Keats.

GREAT ART BEATEN DOWN

Once when Keats and Chapman were staying at Coole, they overheard Yeats making a long distance call to Edmund Dulac. The poet had commissioned the illustrator to provide decorative headings for his latest collection but thought the somewhat décolleté nymphs, whose transparent wings did all too little to conceal their charms, might prove too much for his Irish publisher. He urged the illustrator to re-draw the sprites in less revealing costume. Dulac grew enraged, thundering, 'Non monsieur, mille fois non!', but Yeats slammed down the telephone with an oath. 'One can see the fellow's point,' murmured Keats sotto voce, 'he was doing Yeats a favour, and really our poet has lost a valuable opportunity by this high-handed action.' 'He's cut off his nons to spite his fées,' agreed Chapman.

PEST CONTROL

When Keats and Chapman were studying chemistry, Keats began trying to develop a new sort of insecticide. To his chagrin, all he succeeded in doing was to synthesise a substance that rendered insects invisible. Having poured a fortune into the research, he found himself completely penniless and wandered the city starving and companionless save for a cloud of invisible mosquitoes who had become addicted to his poor thin blood. 'Your friend would appear to have fallen on hard times,' an acquaintance observed to Chapman. 'He doesn't know where his next bite is coming from,' Chapman agreed.

IT PASSED THE TIME

Keats and Chapman were working as pastry chefs in Paris when the Seine broke its banks, and most of their stock floated away on the waist-high waters of the resultant flood. As they splashed about in cold and wet pursuit of fast disappearing cakes and pastries, they bumped into Samuel Beckett. 'What are you doing?' he enquired. 'We're in wading for gateaux,' said Keats testily.

In Memoriam

One day Chapman called on Keats at the funeral parlour where his friend was then employed and found him at the distasteful task of embalming. For this grisly work, Keats explained, he received a fee of £100 per corpse. Chapman in his turn related that he was at work on a biography of the late Douglas de Hyde in which he hoped to portray his subject's human side. Too often had he been painted as the grave and austere ascetic. It was Chapman's laudable wish that he be remembered also as a genial expansive fellow, fond of a jar, a song and a bit of harmless fun. 'That's exactly how I'd like to preserve him myself,' said Keats. 'Informal de Hyde.'

DADA FOR NOW

When Marcel Duchamp came to speak at the philosophical society founded by Keats and Chapman, he talked at length about *The Large Glass* and the role of chance in its construction. After it had been dropped and broken, he incorporated the cracks. And when dust accumulated on its surfaces, he glued that on as well. After the lecture, Duchamp joined the duo in a few large glasses of plain porter before bidding them a good night. When they came down the next day, he had gone, but there was a great pile of dust in the middle of the hall glued to the floor. 'There's nobody like old Marcel,' said Keats, 'I miss his Dadaist antics already.' 'He's left a phil no one can vacuum,' agreed Chapman.

IN THE LAND OF COTTON

Things went swimmingly at first on Keats and Chapman's cotton plantation. They happily contemplated their piles of silver dollars as they chewed their taters and grits and sipped mint juleps, while the contented darkies hummed and ol' man river kept on rollin' along. Of course it was too good to last, and in less time than it takes to tell, a plague of boll weevils reduced them to beggary. As luck would have it, Richard Nixon, then a fresh-faced youth with his future disgrace as yet undreamed of, hit on the plan of opening a vast aquarium in Alabama featuring sharks, dolphins, whales, octopuses and performing seals. He engaged Chapman, but the high-minded Keats would have none of it, deeming it a demeaning and vulgar employment for a dreamer and poet. Chapman's humiliating task was to train white mice to walk on their hind legs in formation while wearing tiny sandwich boards bearing letters to spell out SEA LAND. 'How you can lower yourself in this wise is beyond my comprehension,' scowled Keats, but Chapman drew on his southern dignity and proclaimed defiantly, 'In Dick's Sea Land I'll make mice stand.' 'Away, away,' murmured Keats and, suiting the action to the words, went hurriedly in the other direction.

GOOD TIDINGS

Keats was admiring Chapman's collection of flotsam and jetsam. The undisputed gem of the collection was the figurehead of *The Victory*. Being in festive mood, Keats had brought a bottle of fine champagne with him. Soon both held glasses abrim with winking bubbly. 'To victory,' Keats proposed, indicating the carved figure. 'Can you call to mind a nobler toast?' 'I don't think so,' Chapman replied, 'to the best of my wreck collection.'

The barman in Keats's local, a fierce man for gambling, would bet on anything. Once he removed from beneath the drink-stained counter a faded photograph of his father's sister, an imposing, mustachioed woman in her middle sixties. 'Now lads,' he announced, displaying the portrait, 'what height would say the woman was? If you all put a pound in the kitty, the man as guesses it to the nearest inch will scoop the pool.' All hands being up for the sport, a sum of fifty pounds was raised and deposited in the capacious hat of Keats. Various side bets were covertly placed. As the night wore on, the barman chalked up each guess on the dart score-board. Chapman's estimate was five-foot eleven, but Keats, who claimed to have walked out with the lady in question in the summer of 1896, would have none of it. 'Get him to rub that out and put five-foot two,' he urged. 'You're lowering the aunty,' complained Chapman.

An Odd Fit

When Keats finally lost his marbles, the form his insanity took was the mistaken belief that a cosy miniature saloon bar, complete with staff and customers, had been established in his trousers. Chapman, who was the same size as his old friend, suggested they exchange their nether garments in an effort to dispel this delusion. 'How's that?' he enquired when the swap had been effected. Keats pulled forward his belt and gazed gloomily into his friend's trews. 'Still a little snug in the crotch,' he said sadly.

In the Roaring Twenties

Champions of liberty as they were, none reacted with greater indignation or swifter practicality to the monstrous imposition of prohibition than Keats and Chapman. Within weeks of this high-handed ordinance's institution, the pair and all belonging to them had the biggest bootleg operation on the Lower East Side. Uncles, sisters, brothers, nieces all participated – it was a family affair. After a time, however, Chapman became crazed with ambition for power and began trying to take over everything. He tried to tell everyone exactly what to do, although none of them needed or heeded his advice.

'I already know how to distil water,' Keats's uncle complained. 'There's nothing you can tell me about copper wire that I don't already well know,' his own aunt groaned. At last Keats confronted him in the cooperage, where the senior members of the families busied themselves with the manufacture of all manner of casks and tubs. Keats's grandparents were welding hoops while Chapman's occupied themselves with the woodwork. Chapman began finding fault with the welding. 'Look here, old man,' said Keats, indicating with a graceful gesture his companion's relatives, 'go and teach your granny to saw kegs.'

PUT NOT YOUR TRUST IN PRINCES

After Charles (The People's King) came to the throne, he remained the Milligan-quoting, plant-addressing, jug-eared buffoon we have come to love. When the laureate's position fell vacant, Keats deluged the monarch, through his secretary, with a plethora of applications. All, after the first, were consigned unopened to the wastepaper basket. Undeterred, Keats redoubled his efforts, alas to no avail. One morning, Chapman read in *The Times* that the caring King was scheduled to appear at the local maternity hospital to lecture on folic acid. 'Here's your chance to encounter him in person,' Chapman enthused. Thus, as the King posed for a photo opportunity with a hastily borrowed infant in one hand and a nappy in the other, Keats broke through security and demanded to know why he was being subjected to what amounted to a conspiracy of silence. The King took the safety pin out of his mouth, and dropped the soiled napkin into a portable recycler. 'I'm afwaid I've wather got my hands full just at the moment Mr. err...' he wavered. 'You're changing the subject,' asserted Keats. Everyone held their noses.

PUT TO THE QUESTION

Like Evelyn Waugh, with whom he had often romped when they were but barefoot dead-end kids, Keats had scant time for Americans. Still less did he care for strangers who had the effrontery to call with impertinent demands to have books inscribed or to subject him to a barrage of personal questions for the fashionable press. Judge therefore of his displeasure when, one afternoon while dictating a passage from *Endymion* to the awestruck Chapman, he was interrupted by a thunderous knocking at the front door. Near apoplexy, Keats strode to the door and flung it open to reveal a little man bearing a clipboard. The fellow wore a nasty grey suit of execrable cut. His short hair and wire rimmed spectacles shone with equal brilliance in the bright day.

'Say,' he began in an accent instantly recognisable as originating in the New World, 'ah'm conductin' sort of a survey here and ah surely would appreciate it if you could see your way to answerin' some of these here questions. First off...' But before the fellow could go any further Keats had slammed the door in his face with a graceful oath. His good humour restored, he rubbed his hands together and strolled back to his rapt amanuensis. 'I think I handled that rather well,' he said. 'You put a stop to his Gallup,' said Chapman admiringly.

COUP DE THÉÂTRE

When Chapman was appointed head of the Criminal Investigation Division at Stratford-Upon-Avon, where Keats appeared nightly in the title role of *Richard III*, he decided to attend the first night. As luck would have it, a notorious jewel thief was spotted and apprehended by Chapman, who leapt with the agility of a gazelle from his place of concealment in Richard's cardboard hump and slapped the gyves on the astounded miscreant to a round of well-earned applause from the delighted crowd. 'It's a fair cop, guv,' allowed the miscreant, 'but what sixth sense led you to suspect a penchant for the bard's oeuvre in a ne'er-do-well like yours truly?' 'I was playing a hunch,' explained Chapman.

THAT WILL DO FOR THE PRESENT

It was Christmas morning. Chapman thumbed disappointedly through the slim volume of philosophical essays by noblemen that Keats had given him; Keats admired himself in the looking glass, wearing the handsome smoking jacket he had received from Chapman. 'This isn't much of a present,' Chapman remarked testily. 'It's the Counts that thought,' said Keats.

WHAT THOUGHT DID

Stern rationalist that he was, Chapman scoffed openly when, after a visit to Thoor Ballylee, Keats produced a conch that Yeats had given him through which he hoped to communicate telepathically with his brother poet. There was a small pad of paper inside, and Yeats hoped by intense concentration to cause words to appear thereon from hundreds of miles away. After weeks of failure, Yeats hit on the plan of thinking hard about the sensory organs, so he was delighted when Keats was able to report that the word "rose" had been received. Yeats had been trying to send the word "nose". When, after trying to send the word "mouth" the word "south" appeared, even Chapman was convinced.

One evening Keats had a number of important guests to dinner and left the now fascinated Chapman in charge of the apparatus. Judge of Chapman's excitement when the word "hear" appeared in Yeats's hand. He rushed into the dining room where Keats was just reaching the climax of an after-dinner story. 'Well,' he said testily, as Chapman sidled up, 'what is it?' Chapman bent to whisper, 'A word in your shell like "ear".'

A TRUE SAYING

Although they were receivers of stolen goods so expert as never to have been apprehended, the couple residing next door to Keats were infinitely obliging and otherwise law-abiding citizens. If it was a case of the loan of a lawn mower or a cup of sugar, they couldn't have been more helpful. Chapman pointed out this curious disparity between their lawlessness and a generosity amounting to altruism. 'Good fences make good neighbours,' explained Keats.

How's That?

When Keats and Chapman were at Eton, they accompanied several of their classmates on the school trip to Moscow. While there, they decided to play a cricket match against the local scholars. As chance would have it, the Muscovite team featured a splendid batsman, but in a very short time all the Russian bowlers had come a cropper. As captain, Keats ordered Chapman, the only fluent Russian-speaker of the group, to go off and find some more. 'There's no reds for the wicket,' responded his friend.

LITTLE MEN

Fallen on (all together now) hard times, Keats and Chapman were forced to take on work as assistants in a company manufacturing garden ornaments. Many were the squirrels, hedgehogs, tortoises, etc. that the duo cranked out, often working far into the night to fulfil an order. One day their supervisor presented them with a particularly urgent request for 100 garden gnomes. 'If you get them moulded, painted and delivered to the Botanic Gardens by next Thursday, I'll see to it that there'll be a nice wad of extra cash for youse in yer next pay packet,' the foreman promised.

By working flat out, the industrious pair, much spattered with clay and paints, managed the lot by 11p.m. on the Wednesday. They loaded up the van and set off for their destination the next morning. Keats was driving and, as he approached the traffic lights, decided to take a chance on amber. A Garda car coming from the right slammed into the side of the van and the awful sound of 100 miniature models shattering rent the air. A grim faced sergeant clutching a pencil and notebook strode purposefully toward the van. 'There,' said Keats sadly, 'goes our clay gnomes bonus.'

HARD TIMES

Anxious to make good, the teenage Keats and Chapman worked hard at the Ritz in Belgravia, operating the ancient lift, polishing shoes, cleaning the chimneys, peeling potatoes, walking the guests' dogs, and so on. Another of their duties in those pre-alarm-clock days was to awaken such citizens as had urgent business dealings in the great metropolis. Some awarded generous gratuities for this trifling service, others nothing, variety being, as an old saying has it, "the spice of life".

When the famous cook Mrs. Beeton left a call for 6:30, it fell to the luckless soot-smeared Chapman to rouse the grande dame from her slumbers. The famously irascible old lady rewarded the youth by boxing his ears for his pains. 'It's not fair,' Chapman later complained below stairs to Keats, who was roasting a stale herring over a guttering candle. 'Getting Beeton up is part of life,' he reassured his companion.

LET THEM EAT CAKE

When Keats and Chapman were taken on as apprentice pastry chefs at the Gresham, they were at first entrusted only with the most trifling tasks. In time, however, their artistic potential was realised, and soon their frostings and fillings were a byword wherever cake fans gathered. All the hues of the rainbow flowed from their bowls and blenders; Art Nouveau extravaganzas and the pointillism of hundreds and thousands combined to enchant the eye as well as the palate.

It was, however, on the night of the ball given to celebrate the first solo air-crossing of the Atlantic that the duo achieved their masterpiece. Weeks of planning went into the creation of a full-scale model of the plane in pastry. So scrupulously accurate were our heroes in estimating the amount of ingredients that on the confection's completion there remained no leftover portion to taste, no, not a crumb or a plum. The entire staff waited in an agony of suspense as the enormous comestible was wheeled in to the gasps of the glitterati. A hush fell as Dev cut the first slice. Soon, all that could be heard was the rhythmic champing of a thousand pairs of jaws. Chapman, straining to hear from the kitchen, remarked delightedly to his colleague, 'Listen, Keats, they're chewing our plane.'

LOVE'S OLD SWEET SONG

When Keats attended medical school, he fell for a beautiful girl who studied dermatology. And when she cleared up his painful and disfiguring shaving rash he was more taken with her than ever. 'You see,' he explained, 'I have details of my health relevant to my ophthalmologist under "My Eyes", those relevant to my orthodontist under "My Teeth" and so on.' 'And what about me?' simpered his inamorata. 'I've got you under "My Skin",' said Keats.

ONLY WORDS

By the time the Reverend Spooner visited Keats and Chapman at the farmhouse they were renting, he had become so eccentric that he took to carrying a burning glass about with him everywhere. With the aid of this device he was wont to focus the sun's rays so as to scar numerous items of furniture. These, however, were so old and battered that no remarks were passed.

On one occasion he forgot himself and set ablaze the socks of a visiting Shakespearean expert, Professor Hoffenstein, while that unfortunate gentleman dozed in a deckchair. Another regrettable incident occurred when the farmer from whom they 'rinted' the premises, a highly choleric individual, left his employees' pay packets on the sideboard and returned only just in time to prevent their immolation to Ra by the doddering pyrophile. Yards were given out. This was the last straw, and our heroes admonished their irksome guest as follows: 'Sear no more the feet of the Hun,' counselled Keats. 'Nor the furious rinter's wages,' added Chapman, but the dotard, seeing the two before him so solemn of aspect and fancying himself at a wedding replied, 'I now mispronounce you wan and mife.' One had to laugh.

The Toast of Europe

When Keats and Chapman were on the Grand Tour, they fell under the potent spell of Ben-evenuto Cellini and took to melting down silver coins, which they utilised to fashion exquisite three-dimensional simulacra of everyday objects. The wealthy Venetians, beguiled by the piquant contrast between the precious medium and the quotidian subject matter, vied with one another to obtain specimens of the poets' art. Clothes pegs, mouse-traps, matchboxes – all exquisitely rendered – soon adorned the sideboards and mantelpieces of the fashionable. In time, not unnaturally, word of the artisans' prowess reached the ear of the chief mag-istrate, and the friends were summoned to his palace. One by one, Keats unwrapped a series of miniature marvels. All gasped in astonishment at the bicycle clips, salt cellars, and thimbles, but noth-ing seemed to impress their fastidious host. Chap-man knew, however, that his colleague's masterpiece, a painstaking replication of a toasted cheese sandwich, could not fail to impress him. 'Go on,' he urged Keats, 'let the Doge see the rarebit.'

INNER CONFIDENCE

During the Famine Commemoration of 1947, the Lord Mayor of Dublin put up a prize of £10,000 for the citizen who could eat the most potatoes. Penniless as ever, Keats and Chapman smote their brows to contrive a scheme to net the cash. After much tinkering in his workshop, Keats proudly displayed to the enthralled Chapman a metal box no larger than a thimble, which he placed beside a stone of fine potatoes. 'Stand well back,' he instructed. At lightning speed, the box sprang on the tubers. It opened like a bivalve, disclosing several rows of razor-sharp teeth with which it devoured every scrap of the vegetable feast. 'It is all compressed into that miniscule space by a series of ingeniously miniaturised rollers,' explained Keats. 'But how?' began Chapman. Seizing a glass of water in answer, Keats downed the little machine and the drink in one swift move. 'Now I'm sure to win,' he exclaimed. 'D'you really think so, old man?' enquired Chapman. Keats rubbed his stomach confidently. 'It's in the bag,' he said.

DE MINIMIS

Conventional medicine having failed to alleviate a severe rash contracted by the poet, Keats had recourse to a long list of unconventional remedies. When all else had failed, Chapman enthusiastically recommended homeopathy. A sceptical Keats reluctantly acquiesced. Although it availed him nothing, his innate courtesy impelled him to heap thanks on his old companion for his suggestion. 'But what did you think of the concept?' persisted Chapman. 'It's all right in small doses,' allowed Keats.

Austral Interlude

Keats was renowned for his forgiving nature. Once when he and Chapman were visiting Gough Whitlam's private zoo, a koala sprang out of a eucalyptus and mauled him horribly. Far from retaliating in kind, the poet shared his choc ice with the little creature. 'What a noble nature your friend possesses,' remarked the statesman to Chapman at a barbie afterwards on Bondi Beach. 'He's not the sort to grudge a bear,' agreed Chapman.

THE NIGHT PORTER

While Keats sat up worrying, Chapman spent the evening getting in drinks for a crowd of losers at a low hostelry, after which he was so drunk that nothing would do him but to attempt to win £1,000 in a vulgar contest. A broken-down one-time world wrestling champion promised that amount to any member of the public who could go one round with him. Chapman, fortified as he was by eighteen pints of Guinness, was flung ignominiously out the pub door to land in a tangle of bicycles. 'Where have you been until this hour?' demanded Keats, 'and what have you been doing?' as Chapman strolled in at 2 a.m. much the worse for wear. 'Oh a round and a bout,' he slurred.

Weary of this world and its wicked ways, Keats and Chapman retired to the tranquillity of a Trappist monastery situated on a remote western isle. Here they (Huysmans like) exchanged the mysteries of Art for those profounder mysteries of Faith. Their sandaled feet moved silently on stone flags worn smooth by the passage of brother monks over many centuries. Cool water was their drink, coarse black bread their sustenance. A bell summoned them each day to Prime, Terce, Sext, None, and Compline. No other sound but that of the wind or distant waves or the cries of the sea birds interrupted their meditation.

Judge then of the Abbot's chagrin when he encountered Chapman red-faced and hooting with laughter as Keats, his features in a state of perfect composure, diligently plied his beads. Motioning the peccant novice to follow him, he strode purposefully to his cell where, dispensing necessarily with the rule of silence, he demanded that Chapman discover to him any possible mitigating circumstance for this act of appalling insubordination and want of reverence. 'I can't help it,' confessed the shamefaced Chapman, 'it's the way he tells them.'

Post-Nasal Depression

Chapman had never been happy with his nose, which he often compared when in his cups with that of the gallant Cyrano. After reading *Corridors of Power* with a high fever, he suffered a series of vivid hallucinations in which a miniature version of the family of the author set up house on the bridge of Chapman's noble organ. He drove Keats to distraction with his interminable accounts of their doings. These Keats bore patiently (the martyrs, it has been rightly observed, are those who have to live with the saints), until he could stand no more and recommended that his friend consult Dr. Freud. After several intense sessions, the little Viennese succeeded in ridding Chapman of his delusion, but to his horror, he began to suffer from it himself. 'Ach, this is terrible,' he protested of this ghastly transference. 'Don't I know it,' said Chapman. Then he brightened and added, 'Still, it's Snow's kin off my nose.'

TALKING IN THEIR SLEEP

After his ordination, Keats became terribly popular, visiting the sick and indigent and founding a successful youth-club-cum-bingo hall. His one failing was the quality of his weekly sermon, which often set the entire congregation snoring. Self-assured of his powers of extempore oration, he seldom rehearsed, so that while he tended to begin splendidly, he soon lost track of what he was trying to say. About this difficulty he consulted Chapman. 'Why don't you practise what you preach?' suggested his friend.

When Keats and Chapman took Keats's mother on holiday it was to India, where outside the Taj Mahal the dear old lady accidentally offended a Hindu guru by offering him a sip of her Bovril. The next day, she hired a Model T Ford in which she proposed touring with her son and his faithful companion. Just an hour into their journey, the vehicle blew a tyre. Then another. Moments later, the axles snapped in halves, the radiator boiled over and all the doors fell off. 'Bad car, Ma,' said Keats.

Something Fishy

Many of Keats's most tender lyrics were inspired by the barmaid at his local, The Angler's Rest. The lass was a flame-haired temptress who might have sat for Rubens in another, more gracious, age. Not alone that, but she was herself no mean exponent of the piscatorial art. Too shy to enumerate her obvious physical charms, the poet couched his adoration in metaphor. She was the net in which he was taken, the lure for which he fell, (willingly) gave up his freedom and so forth. Chapman was mystified, for she was in truth a woman of surpassing plainness. One evening as the poet raptly recited his latest tribute, 'Ode on my Beloved's Fishing Rod', the fellow next to Chapman heaved a profound sigh. 'I can't think what he sees in her,' he confided. 'He's fallen for her hook, line and sinker,' said Chapman.

NOSTALGIE DE LA BOUE

High as a brace of kites, our heroes staggered through London Town fuelled by many a late pint of Old Peculiar. As Big Ben rang the third hour, they reeled into a Soho pub almost as lit up as themselves. 'Mud wreshling,' spluttered Keats, stumbling past Peter Stringfellow towards a dingy establishment. 'Tha' looksh li' fun,' Chapman agreed, hiccupping blasts through a toy whistle, though the cardboard policeman's helmet he was wearing obscured the fading photographs of un-draped maidens wallowing like the hippopotami they resembled in glorious mud over which his companion now drooled. Handing £200 to a leer-ing pencil-moustached wide boy in a suit no moth would eat, the two staggered to their sticky ciga-rette-scarred red velvet seats. Soon they were quaffing "Shampagne" (twenty-five quid the sherry glass) in the company of a couple of Siouxsie Sioux lookalikes. When the curtain rose, the girls in the mud pit, so far from being in a state of nature, were clad in oversize pants and halter tops which left everything to the imagination. 'Not even top-less,' sighed a disillusioned Chapman after they were ejected for complaining, 'and we've spent a fortune. What a rip off.' 'Where there's muck there's bras,' agreed Keats sadly.

THE MAN OF STEEL

After he received his degree in painting from the National College of Art and Design, Keats rapidly gained a reputation for his splendid society portraits. As his reputation grew, so alas did his fondness for high living. While working on his portrait of Stalin (at that time the only communist leader to holiday regularly in Ireland, a week below in the Kerry Gaeltacht and another at Mrs. Finnegan's in Sutton on Sea without fail, rain or shine), he went on a bender of astonishing proportions. On the eighth day of this prolonged debauch, Matt Talbot voiced his concern to the poet's old friend. 'He's painting the town red,' said Chapman.

EMINENT EDWARDIANS

Keats and Chapman were taking tea with the Bloomsbury set when the Tardis landed, and out hopped Tom Baker, complete with trademark hat and scarf and really fitting in rather well with the rest of the group. On being asked to sit down and partake of some light refreshment by the formidable author of *To The Lighthouse*, the intergalactic time lord panicked and fled without a word. 'How extraordinary,' remarked Lytton Strachey languidly through his crumpet-crumb-besprinkled beard. 'Who's afraid of Virginia Woolf,' remarked Keats.

A POOR PLAYER

Finding themselves once again in reduced circumstances, Keats and Chapman signed up as extras for the Abbey production of *A Midsummer Night's Dream*. During the production's protracted run, they made the acquaintance of an individual whose situation was even more wretched than their own. The poor fellow was the sole support of a large family and, though naturally given to melancholy, had been cast against type as the jolly weaver in the Bard's immortal romp.

One evening, desperate for a cure, Chapman borrowed the unfortunate fellow's last shilling, which out of the goodness of a simple heart he willingly gave, facing stoically into the spills of icy rain for the ten-mile walk his generosity had necessitated. Keats was appalled at his friend's thoughtlessness. 'This is going beyond the beyonds,' he expostulated. 'How could you stoop to such a mean turn?' 'I've hit Bottom,' admitted the shamefaced Chapman.

The terrible winter of 1854 found Britain and France in uneasy alliance against the Russian Bear, and Keats and Chapman in uneasy alliance against penury, attempting to earn a crust as songwriters. Desperately in need of a hit, they were lighting a fire with the piano stool and a copy of *The Times* when an item about how a British detachment became lost in freezing fog near Balaklava and drowned to a man in the snow-swollen waters of a river in spate caught Chapman's eye. 'The commander died in Florence Nightingale's arms. He was awarded a posthumous V.C.,' he enthused, vamping a suitably funereal riff on the dusty Steinway's nicotine-yellow ivories. 'The thing will write itself,' agreed Keats. 'The public eats up acts of futile gallantry – the Charge of the Light Brigade, Custer's Last Stand, the Battle of Thermopylae, you know the shtick. We'll have a smash on our hands for sure.' 'But what to call it?' mused Chapman aloud. 'A catchy title is a must.' 'How about "Crimea River"?' suggested Keats.

'Twas the season to be jolly but, alas, scant jollity was in evidence chez Keats, where that worthy sat huddled over a little smoky fire while his old friend foraged for fuel. Moments later Chapman entered, his thinning hair dusted with snow, bearing a single sodden briquette. Keats took Chapman's chilly, fingerless-gloved hands in his warm ones saying, 'Minus ten.' 'How can you tell the temperature so accurately?' asked Chapman through chattering teeth. 'Oh, I've always been able to do that,' explained Keats, 'it's a family gift.' He removed a slab of cold porridge from the now bare larder and they made a frugal meal.

Suddenly inspired, Chapman threw on his coat, bade Keats do likewise, and dragged his friend protesting into the icy night. 'But what ... ' he was saying as they shouldered their way through the throng of last-minute shoppers. 'Look!' cried Chapman triumphantly. They stood before a brightly-lit shop window. Animatronic elves sang in Disney-mouse voices, dancing through cardboard snowdrifts and Styrofoam storms about a hamper of good things. A turkey, an enormous ham, pounds of prime sausages, a great Christmas pudding, a large iced cake and bottle upon bottle of fine malt whiskey and vintage port enticed the frozen friends. Above the bounty a rainbow of neon letters spelled out the legend "Win this grand prize. Guess Frosty's temperature."

Grinning from a refrigerated cabinet was the jovial snowman adverted to with a carrot nose and shining coal black eyes. But our heroes' eyes out-shone them now. 'How cool is that?' asked Chapman.

Not with a Bang

When Keats and Chapman took up archery, they were too impoverished to equip themselves with targets. Fortunately, T. S. Eliot gave them a couple of old cheeses, and soon they were to be seen in their back garden happily pegging away at these odorous wheels, gossiping idly as they perfected the ancient discipline. Eliot, happening by to find out what progress they were making, enquired with characteristic politeness whether their conversation was of a private nature or whether, if it were general, he might be accorded the pleasure of joining in. 'Certainly you may,' said Keats civilly, 'we're just shooting the bries.' Eliot whimpered dimly in the calid afternoon.

A Happy Ending

Having hitchhiked to Canada to pan for gold, Keats and Chapman were soon broke. Chapman hit on the suggestion that they engage as lumberjacks and amass a collection of rare woods to sell at a profit in New York. This they set about and with such success that within weeks, they had filled their beat-up second-hand aeroplane with a huge pile of mahogany. Judge therefore of their irritation when the weight proved too much for the motor.

All seemed lost until Keats encountered an eccentric who had built a light aircraft of his own from ponderosa logs felled on the same plantation and was determined to fly it to New York. 'Jest attach your crate to mine an' I'll haul you clear to them bright lights, pardners,' he dribbled round his pipe in authentic frontier gibberish.

Our heroes, complying eagerly, were soon airborne and relaxing in the cockpit of their over-loaded craft. 'Isn't this great?' said Chapman. 'We're on our way to a golden fortune thanks to this fellow's ingenious scheme.' 'A pine tow-plane is your only man,' said Keats.

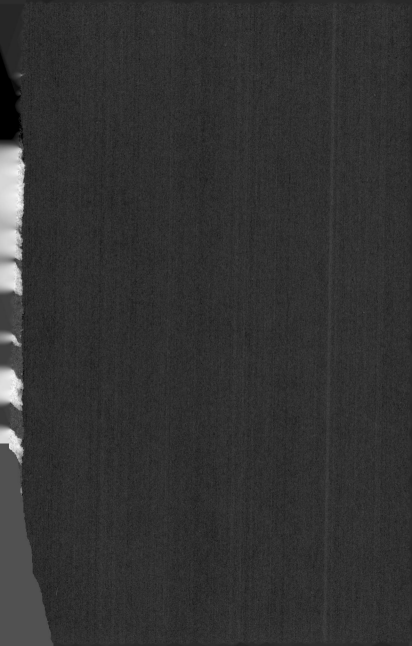

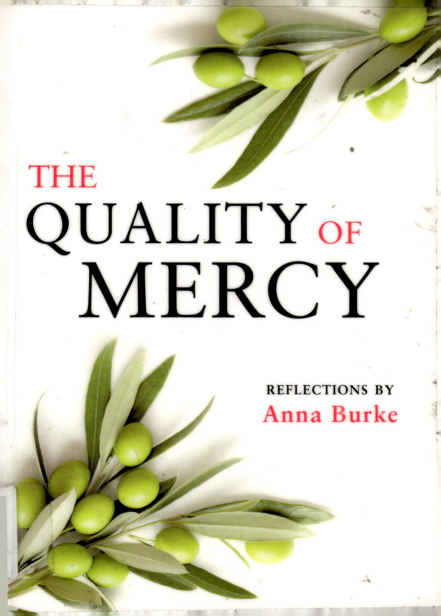

THE
QUALITY OF
MERCY

REFLECTIONS BY
Anna Burke

THE QUALITY OF MERCY

Anna Burke is a Sister of Mercy. She has worked in education and faith development in Florida, Zambia, South Africa and Ireland. Her previous publications includes *When Silence Falls: The Stations of the Cross* (2008), *In the Secret of My Heart: Moments of Stillness in the Heart of Christ* (2010) and *While They Where at Table: Eucharistic Prayers and Reflections* (2012), all published by Veritas.

THE
QUALITY OF
MERCY

REFLECTIONS BY
Anna Burke

VERITAS

Published 2015 by
Veritas Publications
7–8 Lower Abbey Street
Dublin 1, Ireland
publications@veritas.ie
www.veritas.ie

ISBN 978 1 84730 636 4

10 9 8 7 6 5 4 3 2

A catalogue record for this book is available from the British
Library.

Cover design by Heather Costello
Printed in the Republic of Ireland by SPRINT-print Ltd, Dublin

*Veritas books are printed on paper made from the wood pulp of
managed forests. For every tree felled, at least one tree is planted,
thereby renewing natural resources.*

TABLE OF CONTENTS

WHAT ARE YOU LOOKING FOR?
John 1:38

People ask me from time to time, 'What are you looking for?' The rooting in the drawer, the urgency of the search, the total preoccupation – it all provokes the question. In fact, few other things engage us the way searching does. In our culture, despite the fact that gadgetry and technology make almost everything available at the touch of a button, we are frantic with searching. In this time of overkill, the search has intensified as the lost treasure sinks into the data pile. At critical moments we come face to face with losing and finding, with light and darkness, with fear and peace. This struggle is at the very heart of human longing as we seek to discover meaning in the ultimate questions of life and death, and the roadway in between.

The first words of Jesus in John's Gospel are about the great search. 'What seek ye?' Jesus is addressing the deepest human longing which will shape the birthing of Christian discipleship. He is taking the first steps in the story of every relationship – what are we looking for? Everyone dreams the dream but the search uncovers what we never imagined. Jesus would lead his people into questions and uncertainties, into knowing and unknowing, through storms to the mountain top.

Life is the rhythm of losing and finding; every little search reflects the yearning for completion stirring the heartbeat of all creation. The lost key and the lost phone connect us with the great unlocking of the evolving mystery. What am I really looking for? Phrases like 'Someone in the great Somewhere, Searching for me', come to mind. With all creation we groan for the Oneness that is mercy.

Searching is part of the journey and the human search fills the pages of history. From the lost key to lost direction, our ongoing search is intense, leaving us sometimes bewildered, sometimes distressed, but always grasping. We search in the wrong places, in unlikely places and in life-giving places. The evidence is there, in archaeological sites, in ancient art, in today's pilgrimage. Without back-up texts or religious creeds the primal human urge to touch something or someone beyond the visible limits is embedded in burial places, in stone, in design that sought to face the rising sun.

WHERE DO YOU LIVE?
John 1:38

What is it about directions in Ireland? In a small country like ours, getting directions can be quite a problem. We tend to require some vital statistics before the map is revealed. The answer to the 'where is it?' question becomes very complicated, especially when directions are given by landmarks and house colours and even the route not to take! In truth, getting to one's destination is as much about personal choice as it is about directions. We can take the high road or the low road or the by-road or the no road. 'Where do you live?' can be a difficult question to answer.

In John's Gospel, Jesus responds to the question with an invitation to come to his home and see for ourselves. There is something special about the invitation to come home. It was a birth moment for the Christian community. Jesus understood their need to place him somewhere, to find his roots, to meet the family. When they asked, 'where do you live?' they were beginning the journey into discipleship, making the connection that was to outlast time. The way to find Jesus is to go home with him. We need the information that roots give – the family school, the village tree, the source of the heartbeat, the mercy that defines the relationships. In Jesus' home, the directions are clarified and we begin to see the road ahead.

Homes are revealing places. They tell us about the character of relationships, how the threads of close bonds are woven. The stones and streets and hedges and grasses reveal human presence. They become our story, holding our memories, recording our journeys. Home is where the heart comes to know itself, to hear its own longings and to experience its capacity for mercy. When they asked 'where do you live?' they were seeking the inside story of the one who called them. In the place he called home they would pick up the identity of love. At the table they would share his bread and drink from his cup. Home would answer their questions about the journey ahead, about the starting point and the destination. From home we came, to home we will return.

Some people can never return home. When we ask them 'where do you live?' they are silent, sometimes confused. They cannot reconcile home with the dream that died and the shadow that deepened. Although a home that betrays us is intolerable, the desire to go back is a constant yearning. We long to cross the threshold and be one again. Good or bad, home is indelible and in an extraordinary way homes are about mercy; they always take us in. 'Come and see.'

WHO ARE YOU?
John 8:25

Getting to know somebody can arouse a series of mixed emotions. If the person is not as bad as we had imagined there is a sense of relief, but if we have doubts there is a feeling of unrest, even fear. Oddly, it seems mistrust can come from good coverage as well as from bad coverage. The question in John 8:25 indicates that the authorities were seriously concerned about the identity of Jesus and the impact of that identity.

They knew his name and his address and his accent. We can assume that they had meticulously collated all the biographical data available, but this information did not define him. As leaders in political, social and religious circles the authorities felt threatened by this man who was drawing the people to a new way of thinking and assessing. They were grappling with the 'who are you?' question that seemed to stand between them and the man from Galilee. The very question was his great contribution to time, to our time, shining an unquenchable light on the identity of Jesus. Being without an impressive education, family prestige or political influence he was still gathering the crowds, opening eyes and ears, changing the power structure. The people found something incredibly attractive about him and they gathered where he stopped, and followed him to the mountains and listened to his voice. It was like the pull of gravity, the touch of mercy after centuries of law enforcement.

The priests and the Levites couldn't handle the *who*. It was so out of reach, yet so present; so harmless, yet so powerful; so obvious, yet so mysterious, that they were disturbed at their unknowing. Worst of all, he drew the largest crowds. He unnerved their system by his stillness and unravelled it by his teaching. But it was surely his mercy that eventually uprooted their empire! With his presence he did what the armies of Rome had failed to do: he forgave the sinner and the accuser. Who are you?

There comes a time in every life to ask the *who* question. This is the survivor in us, the essential part. *Who* is the link word, from the morning of life to its close, the deciding factor. *Who* expresses the human capacity, the quality of choice, the depth of awareness. When they asked 'who are you?' they beheld the magnificence of mercy and the unveiling of the cosmic attraction.

HOW DO YOU KNOW ME?
John 1:48

The question 'how do you know me?' opens up the ancient biblical story of the One who was with God in the beginning. This question is about the remembering of God. 'I will never forget you.' It is pointing us to the First Light, to the God who knew us before we were born, whose love called us forth from the earth into the eternal lifeline. We, who came forth from the divine breath, are enfolded in mercy from the beginning. We were in the heart of God at daybreak, at the dawning of the day. The question from Nathaniel is about a genetic line.

'I know you from somewhere!' We have all had that experience of sensing a connection with someone. Jesus knew Nathaniel, his potential and his quality of spirit. Beyond the hearsay he looked deeply into the heart of the man. Nathaniel's question puts a spotlight on our understanding of seeing. Like Nathaniel we also define people by address and reputation, and we have all asked if anything good can possibly come from Nazareth. Unfortunately prejudice can rob us of the best moments in life and shut down the encounters that make a difference. Nathaniel was caught in the trap of transmitted perception and Nazareth came between him and Jesus. In finding Jesus, however, he discovered that social prejudice blurs our vision and distorts our assessments. Mercy does not have borders; as Nathaniel approached Jesus he was greeted with open arms. Jesus sees the best in us; he cut through the layers and saw the 'man without guile'. A new way of seeing was proclaimed.

'How do you know me?' Nathaniel is amazed. Jesus has named the essence of the man and that is the quality of mercy. It is a profound moment in every life when someone gets it right about us, thus ending our isolation. There is no deeper longing than to love and be loved, just as we are. Isolation is a dark place and separation is extinction. Someone has found him! Someone has recognised a likeness, a kinship. Nathaniel is claimed as God's own; the search is over. Mercy is like that, the all-seeing lens, the vision that rescues us from public perception. It reaches out to the real person, to the heart beyond the fence.

We hear in the Nathaniel story how meeting Jesus changes how we see people. The carpenter from Nazareth, a place of ill repute, became for Nathaniel a life-altering presence. For the first time in John's Gospel we witness the dramatic transformation that happens when our way of seeing changes: 'You are the Son of God; You are the King of Israel.' Nathaniel was freed; he had met the Christ and was seeing again.

IS THERE NO ONE LEFT TO CONDEMN YOU?

John 8:10

The late Nelson Mandela embodied the dynamic between the oppressor and the oppressed. When condemnation ceases the oppressed and the oppressor go free. Pope Francis has returned us to this awareness in his rejection of condemnation within the Christian ethic. The Gospel story reveals the person of God in Jesus as the One who forgives, who longs for reconciliation, who is without condemnation. Jesus was not against the law; he was against an interpretation of the law that imprisoned the hearts and minds of the people.

We usually think of the law as the great arbitrator. It is the authority of the land and it is neither acceptable nor advisable to challenge it. Therefore, in many ways the law takes on an infallible dimension, although the verdict doesn't always mean that justice has been served. Jesus understood the role of the law but he gave it a new quality. It was a way of invitation rather than enforcement, of healing rather than hurting, of mercy rather than punishment. This was a daring leap in the law-driven society of his time. Jesus took on the law! He didn't condemn it; he merely exposed it and the truth became his penalty.

As the woman stood before the stoning squad, Jesus saw in the execution of justice the relationship between the sin that is discovered and the sin that is hidden. He was unveiling a rare insight into the delicate balance between condemnation and scapegoating. His action in defence of this woman was a marker for the law. The badge of 'criminal', both then and now, always mirrors the hidden layers. Criminalising the victim lets all of us off the hook.

Is there no one left to condemn you? This particular moment in biblical history saw the pendulum swing from the woman's sin to the woman's love, from the law of condemnation to the mercy of God. As he wrote their sins in the sand that day, Jesus confirmed a cosmic movement. The law required a different question to verify the evidence. The criminal required another hearing, where the one without sin passed sentence.

ARE YOU GOING TO WASH MY FEET?
John 13

Peter's surprise is no surprise! His question reflects how most of us think some of the time. The status of service, especially the kind that gets down on the ground to feet level, is frequently demoted on the social scales. Peter is obviously struggling with this radical shake-up of the old world order. Jesus sees that a gap in understanding is now a potential separation point between himself and Peter. Peter is a product of a culture of class distinction where rabbis, emperors and governors rule from a throne. It is unimaginable for him that the one he proclaims as Messiah is talking about washing the dirty, scarred and disfigured feet of a fisherman.

It is difficult to relearn the lessons of a lifetime, but changing an ages old mindset is part of life's journey. Peter's question, with all its disbelief, is a revelation. In this moment of resistance we are all facing the unveiling of the great truth that the totally compassionate one, the merciful one, the ruler of heaven and earth has emptied himself to become the servant. The world is turning upside down before his very eyes. Whoever heard of a servant king? Peter has to move!

Are you going to wash my feet? Are you going to come down to my level? Are you going to hold in your hands the feet that have known the grime and dirt, the sewers and alleyways of this land? Are you actually thinking of kissing these feet and wrapping them in a linen towel? On the other hand, a relationship of this kind, the heart-to-heart kind, depends on real knowing, on 'getting' the other person. Relationships break up all the time when hidden information comes to light, so it is better to get things clear from the start, especially the issue of spiritual compatibility.

All of this questioning is going on at the table of the meal. We have been told many times that Eucharist is what we become and this amazing visual of the table food and the man with the towel speaks to us of Eucharist as a life-altering encounter, a life for the life of the world. The gift of the servant is the gift of life. The table and the towel are inseparable. The Messiah and the servant are in a blood covenant. In the hour of Passover, as the shadows of evening gathered and every relationship held its breath, Peter saw the implications of a disciple's promise and he opened his arms to the world. 'Not only my feet, but also my hands and my head.' Their relationship written on a towel became timeless.

ARE YOU ONE
OF THE DISCIPLES?
John 18:17

When I was growing up, the Church was seen to be all-powerful and we learned from a very early age to fear God. God was always watching, ready to pounce and ever ready to punish. As we grew older some of us came to understand that fear of God was the lesser of two evils … and as we grew older still we came to see that mercy and fear do not coexist. Today, things have changed and fear is now rooted in public opinion, in newspaper reporting, in political opportunism and in financial greed. At least God had a forgiving system …

The girl who questions Peter is really interested in Peter's God. She is looking at his identity in terms of his association. The value system he has linked into is a greater threat to the establishment than Peter's ethnic origins. We are known by the company we keep and the things we live and die for defy disguise. What was it about Peter that drew the girl to him? The story seems to imply that she picked him out. There is always a price to be paid for identifying with a group, and when we enrol we reflect in our person the values we have chosen.

Group identity is not always a cause of crucifixion. Some groups are safe havens with protection from the mightiest. Other groups are safe havens because they are essentially silenced by the mightiest. There are also groups that protect the mightiest and these are as safe as you can get. Peter was silenced; somehow he knew the penalty if found guilty by the ruling crowd. He knew that it was better for him to cover up and shut up. Peter helps us to understand the power of fear in our battle for freedom of speech and freedom of belief.

Assessment by public opinion is a very frightening prospect. Two thousand years is a short time and today many people still live, frozen, in the fear of identification.

WHICH OF THESE WAS A NEIGHBOUR?
Luke 10:36

We usually think of neighbours as those who live next door or nearby. Local geography and neighbours fit together. Neighbours know us; they know what the forensics never uncover – the whole story. Without credentials to prove it, they become part of the extended family, turning up at all the critical moments of life. Neighbours excel at being there. The neighbour in Luke's Gospel, however, was a stranger and this immediately undermines our definition.

The Samaritans were a very unwanted people and the man from Samaria, in addition to being a stranger in the locality, was separated by history, ancestry and values from the local understanding of neighbour. He carried on his shoulders the suspicion of the locals. He is the one whose help is neither sought nor wanted. His presence is seen to lower the value of the property and to reduce the status of the neighbourhood. It wasn't just a brave gesture to get down on the ground and pick up the Jewish man; it was an act of mercy.

Samaria is everywhere … In his Lenten Message of 2015, Pope Francis spoke of the 'globalisation of indifference' in the world today. The pope is calling us to confront the attitude of *global proportions* that attends only the self, and neglects people who are living in poverty. Pope Francis cautions us about taking 'refuge in a universal love that would embrace the whole world while failing to see Lazarus sitting before our closed doors'. When Jesus asks us to identify the one who was neighbour he is expanding our understanding of neighbour and challenging our mindset.

Neighbours are always aware, ever vigilant. Their vision is within reach. They are the people who put personal danger, reputation and cultural habits on hold. Neighbours jump in for us; they reach through the danger and search through the fumes. Neighbours are the answer to the concern of Pope Francis because they are incapable of indifference and unafraid of restrictions.

Which of the three was neighbour? It has to be the one who beat indifference.

WHY DO YOU SEE THE SPECK IN YOUR NEIGHBOUR'S EYE?
Luke 6:41

Most of us excel in diagnosing others. We know their reasons, their motives and especially their weak points. Our assessment of other people is usually *spot on* and we have no shortage of remedies that will repair their damaged personalities. Seeing specks could be an Irish phenomenon too! When the sun shines we say it is dangerous on the skin and when the clouds gather we say it will be like that for the next six months. The speck is me!

To condemn is easy, a no-skill action. To forgive is divine, the noblest action. Mercy is a way of seeing and it doesn't see specks. There is physical seeing and there is spiritual seeing and they are both subject to blurring; distance from the source restricts all seeing. Spiritual seeing, like physical seeing, varies for each person and when our spiritual sight is no longer serving us well we need a different lens. Mercy is a great visual remedy, a lens with inside focus. Mercy softens the glare and gets behind the scales. It is the inner eye of compassion and it changes specks into human stories and unveils the struggles and efforts and tears.

The specks in my neighbour's eye are frequently the unshed tears of human struggle. Mercy sees the tears longing to be free and it loosens the stones until the river flows. But what about justice? Surely specks have to be accounted for? In his proclamation of the Jubilee Year of Mercy (*Misericordiae Vultus*, 11 April 2015), Pope Francis asks us to ponder the reality that without mercy there is no justice. Mercy and justice are, the pope says, 'a single reality'. Why do you see the speck?

WHAT MIRACLE CAN YOU PERFORM?
John 2:18

In this age of assessment we are learning more and more about the things that cannot be assessed. We are also learning the hard way that criteria have failed us in Church and State. In regard to Jesus, there was an ongoing investigation into his credentials because for a man who was making an impact he had very little to show, on paper at least. His CV was non-existent. The leaders in the temple and in the courtyard wanted something measurable, visible, external. Proof was needed to establish once and for all the identity of this man: 'what miracle can you perform?'

Proof is the agent of science. Absence of proof is the agent of religion. These two approaches need each other for ongoing advancement and expansion. If proof is our only reality, however, then we are surely living in solitary confinement. On the other hand, if absence of proof has no scientific reference point, then we are living apart from reason. 'What miracle can you perform?' The question hits at the very heart of a reality beyond proof. They were struggling to make sense of a man beyond boundaries, beyond the confines of the visible. His miracles were everywhere and yet his greatest miracle was mercy; this one was difficult to grasp and it was changing the course of history right before their eyes.

The miracle of mercy was changing the system and attracting the people. There were mass rallies on the mountain, on the shore, in the valley, everywhere. It wasn't a question of politics; it was a question of mercy. Jesus offered another way of thinking, of living, of believing. He discovered voiceless people on tree tops, in the synagogue and at funerals. He recognised them and called them by name. The criteria were changed forever and the shape of power was turned upside down. The mercy miracle shredded the evidence and forgave the crime. It is so far from our basis of operation that we have no words.

We all desire miracles because they connect us with someone beyond ourselves. Part of our assessment of God is around signs and wonders, someone above and beyond, over and above. Jesus, however, was within and beside and before and behind. His presence with us was mercy – the miracle – from age to age.

HOW CAN YOU ASK ME
FOR A DRINK?
John 4:9

'Can I buy you a drink?' Whatever the answer may be, the question is always an ice-breaker leading to a conversation. Families share cups all the time and drinking from the common cup is a gesture of intimacy and close connection. There is something special and sacred in the shared drink. Jesus, who brought up the idea of a shared drink, had no vessel, and the woman at the well was faced with a predicament – the one of drinking from the same cup. He was a Jew and this level of connection was forbidden by law.

The scene has a familiar ring. We see two people faced with the divisions that separate them. Who will step out and change the history that divides? Who will break the ice of prejudice and irrational fear? Jesus took a giant leap; he asked a Samaritan woman for a drink. Talk about risking a reputation! He wanted water. He wanted a life connection. This encounter was about life. He had crossed over to find her and he pointed her to the water of life. In receiving the water from the well, he was offering her the living water of relationship. Relationships that last are about giving and receiving.

The success of the meeting at the well in Samaria depended on two people who were willing to unchain themselves from the legacy of the past and make a new beginning. A very simple gesture broke the silence of a century. Some might call it a prophetic stance; others might say it was the triumph of mercy. Mercy takes risks because it is fuelled from the heart, drawn, not driven, given and received.

WHERE CAN WE BUY ENOUGH FOOD?

John 6:5

Hunger is an unavoidable human pain and it affects every aspect of our lives. With all creation we are groaning for a relief from hunger. Our hearts were made for God. The great paradox of this pain seems to be that the hungriest people are those who have too much bread. We search for a lifetime to find the right food just to ease the yearning; however, when we are satiated with many things, the intensity of the hunger can worsen. We may resort to desperate measures, even trying hostile substances to numb the emptiness. Where can we get enough?

The apostles, when faced with a huge crowd of hungry people, proceeded to address the symptom; they needed fast food, fast! The gathering, however, was pointing to the underlying cause. They had come out in their thousands because they had sensed the end of famine and the beginning of relief and they sat down and waited. This was the meeting place of the two great hungers, where body and spirit become one. Something happened that day; everyone was satisfied – men, women and children. When this kind of abundance is available to everyone we turn our eyes to the source. The event is a wake-up call for us to reflect deeply on the rights of everyone to partake from the source, both spiritual and physical. The story connects the collective hungers and demonstrates that we share a common responsibility for the distribution of bread.

The question has deep resonance today. As we continue to go along with destructive overconsumption, we are steadily moving towards disaster. The looting of natural resources from the poorest nations in order to gorge financial giants and consolidate wealth in the hands of the few – this is a question of bread. It is a question of the right to bread, sustenance and quality of life. The right to life is about sharing bread. The question is calling us, at least, to a food revolution, to an earth-altering movement in the sharing of bread.

HOW CAN THIS MAN GIVE US HIS FLESH TO EAT?
John 6:52

Language is limiting and words are inadequate most of the time. It is little wonder that the words of Jesus about giving his flesh for our food caused a fair degree of misgiving. But as we explore the words, we see that giving one's flesh is not that unusual. Mothers do it and fathers do it and neighbours and friends do it. When we translate the words into a handing over of unconditional love then the flesh becomes the bond of connection, the covenant of relationship. To give at this level is to identify totally with someone, to share the form and substance of the other. The question in itself points to the unbelievable, to the unimaginable. In the context of the Gospel story, with his violent death already in process, the words of Jesus explain the potential of human history.

The desire to give life, to sustain it and to bring it to fullness is the great energy moving all creation to completion, calling all things to the centre. The raindrops disappear into the earth and the sun nurtures the forests. The pelicans risk the frozen Arctic to feed their young, and the lioness puts her body between the venomous snake and her young cubs. People jump into rivers, walk into infernos to save a life. The flesh of God is our flesh too. Risking life and limb to feed new life is the divine urge alive in us. Self-giving is the law of evolution, the essential human heartbeat.

The words of Jesus about giving his flesh for the world provoked the people's 'how?' How can someone rejected, hammered to the ground, do something like this for his assailants? How can mercy reach such proportions? How can someone see into the abyss of our darkness and stay with us until the dawn? Mercy is measureless. Jesus' gift takes us beyond understanding, beyond words. This is God's thirst, unveiling the Oneness in the flesh of all creation. Self-giving does that; it takes us beyond the limits.

In the Eucharist we come face to face with the reality of the flesh of Christ given for the life of the world. If Eucharist is what we receive and what we become, then we see in this act of emptying the magnificence of the divine presence in human flesh. In his giving, Jesus unveiled the pinnacle of human nature, the wonder of a human heart.

WHY ARE YOU AFRAID?
Mark 4:40

Although we tell ourselves that *God is love* and all creation reminds us of this in visible and magnificent ways, it seems to be an ongoing question mark on life's journey. Sometimes we are sure and at other times we waver. There are times too when the silence of God is too deafening and we just part company. The image of a loving God always exists for us against the backdrop that is the reality of our lives. In the shadows of war and hatred, violence and cruelty, hunger and disease, starvation and waste, we question God. I do not think that God is upset with questioning. In fact, the biblical narrative is a slow painstaking journey of darkness into light, of questioning into discovery. It was never that clear.

If we were to take up the question with God about love as the essence of divine nature, we might be invited again to see ourselves as agents of love, a people who transmit the energy of love. The darkness in our relationships, locally and globally, which results in anguish and disintegration, is hardly God's fault. The balance and harmony of creation was disrupted by us. We are afraid of ourselves. We are afraid of what we have done.

Jesus asked the apostles: 'why are you afraid?' Against the background of a storm and the obvious threat to their lives, this difficult question is asked. Until we give a reason for our fear it controls us. Why were the disciples afraid? The question seems to stand at the junction of life and death. Was there anyone, someone, in their line of vision, who was beyond fear? Had they defined life in terms of their own understanding and capacity to know? Why were they unable to calm the waves? The conversation in every storm, though short and simple, is searching and silencing.

'Why are you afraid?' It's a life-altering question, the beginning of release. Fear is the great destructor of every aspect of life. It silences creative expression, relationships, dreams, rivers and ecosystems; even truth itself dies in the fear.

DO YOU SEE THIS WOMAN?
Luke 7:44

Some people are 'an example to us all', or so we say. When giving examples we tend to hold up the best, and these are usually found in the ordinary events of life. What did this woman do that made her extraordinary? She changed the protocol and rewrote the rules of etiquette, showing us how the established order needs another voice. It's one thing to dream of liberation but another thing completely to take action, open the door and walk out. This was far beyond a protest gesture of a woman in a man's world; it was a transformative action. There were no political points, just a woman walking into a room. The Queen of England bowed her head. The neighbour leaned across the garden fence and shook my hand. The champion runner slowed down to help his friend across the finish line. The soldier crossed the enemy line to sing 'Silent Night'. Do we see these people?

Do you see this woman? She is breaking through. Some modern commentators might call it the evolution of consciousness. Others might say it was the action of prophecy. She seems, however, to have had little else on her mind beyond sheer delight – the simple joy of welcoming, of embracing the one who is loved. Love is the movement, the magnetic energy. Love changes everything! It changes the way we see and hear and respond. It changes the way we lead and serve. It is most profound in the simplest gestures – in the disarmed approach, in the abandoned fear, in the courage of the risk.

The woman in the question is opening the curtain on the dominant culture. She is offering another possibility and drawing us into a new way of feasting. Her silence is informative and her focus is unwavering. It is an exposed place for a woman, surrounded by a respectability and protocol designed by the hands of status and prestige. 'Do you see this woman?' She is channelling the question of mercy through the established order.

Love dismantles barriers and reveals human freedom. It is fearless in its intensity and faithful in its mercy. On her knees and with her tears, the woman wrote a new script and opened a window on the darkness. Now, wherever his story is told it will be called mercy and what she did that day will be remembered.

WHERE IS YOUR FAITH?
Luke 7:26

Faith is learned, at least when it comes to the everyday things. We have no faith in some cars but there are other models we have driven for a lifetime. Faith or the lack of it is also revealed in the clothes we buy and in the food we eat. Although we are all vulnerable to the voice of marketing, faith is not inclined to change position, falling into the 'tried and tested' category. So faith has something to do with influence.

Jesus wondered if there would be any faith left on Earth when he returned. Faith is revealed in the culture; culture is revealed in faith. Doubt is everywhere today because what it says on the tin is no longer convincing. Maybe the Jesus question becomes clearer in times of uncertainty because this is when we yearn for an anchor. In a world where, as Pope Francis has warned, the *globalisation of indifference* threatens the survival of humanity, only faith in God, the Holy Oneness, can restore the connection.

On the sea that day, there was a storm. The men were afraid. They could only see the storm, the immediate, the little space of the boat. 'Where is your faith?' is really a question about trusting the anchor. He was asking them the ultimate question about trust and whether it was strong enough to survive the waves. If this friendship meant anything it would surely stand firm in the storm. They would have to grasp that his presence with them was unsinkable, irremovable. There are moments like this in every relationship, when the trust question is asked and we hold our breath and wait for the answer.

Wouldn't you think God would do something in the storms of life? Why the silence? Why the apparent indifference? Why the suffering of innocent people? Why the triumph of violence and war? The earthquake is not fixed from the outside. The tsunami is not stilled from the shore. Floods are not dried up with mops. The resolution comes from within the disaster. So maybe he is in the storm, and maybe freedom from fear is within the storm.

One thing we can say is that storms reshape us. No one has ever come through a storm unchanged. Storms are never mere events; they are always life-changing experiences. It is only when the wind settles that we tend to hear the voice that held us together. Faith is not about the disaster; it is about the relationship. God is always breaking through. The seed that I buried in the darkness of the earth is breaking through in a tiny stem. The daylight that gave way to night is breaking through in a full moon. The words of mercy are breaking through on the global battlefield. From the storm, God is calling the universe.

WHO TOUCHED ME?
Luke 8:45

Strange things happen where crowds of people gather. Some of us push and shove or jostle for position. A question like 'who touched me?' seems pointless in such a situation. However, in the Gospel of Luke, a whisper sounded through the crowd.

The woman who touched the hem of Jesus' garment reveals the holiness of touch. The earth has been touched by God; humans certainly have not touched it in a holy sense. We touch relics, stones, religious objects, to give and to receive. It is a sacred communication. Religious expression devoid of touch is inanimate and abstract. Pope Francis in *Evangelii Gaudium* (123–6) has encouraged us to respect devotional prayer because communication is more than words and prayer is more than theory. The pope is drawing our awareness to the importance of the whole person – body and spirit – engaging in prayer time. The woman in the crowd needed the devotional touch in order to say her deepest prayer.

We have always held that actions speak louder than words, and in times of great human emotion we find release in the lighted candle, the bunch of flowers, the mementos. We hug, hold on, lean on and stand side by side. Actions allow us to penetrate the silence when words have died. In Irish tradition the great gestures of carrying the coffin, shaking the holy water and walking the pilgrim way are the symbols of a nation in prayer.

Jesus' question is interesting. 'Who touched me?' In this particular crowd scene of pushing and shoving, Jesus is making a much-needed distinction between shove and touch. What did the woman do that was different? She related to his person, valued his holiness and witnessed his mercy. Her touch had the hallmarks of tenderness, gentleness and respect. It was for her an avenue to healing, to freedom and to life. 'Who touched me?' Who connected with me? Who believed in me? Who brought out the best in me? It was a loving touch.

WHAT DO YOU DO WHEN YOU LOSE A SHEEP?
Luke 15:4

What do you do when you lose something? Luke 15 is the *losing and finding* chapter. In an effort to explain the mercy of God, Jesus uses the image of finding and losing. You can't have one without the other. Jesus builds the question slowly, with rare intensity, drawing us in to the experience of shepherding, of going in search of something. What is it about losing and finding that tells us something about God? It is the sheep and shepherd factor.

When some of us were growing up, saints were mysterious people, superhuman. Although we desired to emulate them, the standard seemed unattainable as we tend to see ourselves, most of the time, as lost sheep. In more recent times, however, becoming a saint has taken on an ordinary aspect. Now some of the people we knew, people who walked like us and talked like us and stumbled like us are in the realms of the angels. Shepherding, after all, is about ordinary people going out to search.

Many of us remember St John XXIII. His remarkable quality was ordinariness, and his impact on the twentieth century was remarkable. Saint John XXIII was born into poverty and he grew to understand the Church as the Church of the people. This in particular inspired and informed the Second Vatican Council. 'Good Pope John' worked all his life to save the victims of prejudice and injustice. His Christmas Day visit, in 1958, to the notorious 'Queen of Heaven' prison in Rome, revealed the person behind the role. As he embraced an old man with a lengthy prison sentence, John XXIII was heard to say, 'I have looked into your eyes with my eyes. I have put my heart near your heart.' They found one another that day, the shepherd and the sheep. Let there be mercy!

The news of the beatification of Óscar Romero on 23 May 2015 was received with great joy. The former Archbishop of San Salvador gave his life for his people, torn apart by war, defaced by inequality. Óscar Romero did what few of us dare to do: he held the political establishment to account. When his close friend, Rutilio Grande, a Jesuit priest, was murdered, the archbishop named the military government of San Salvador as conspirators in his death and he called for an investigation and prosecution. The Church hierarchy turned against him for alienating the political establishment. Death threats followed and the ordinary man who interpreted the Gospel in terms of liberation for the forgotten sheep was shot dead on 24 March 1980. Shepherds die for their sheep. His beatification renews our hope in the voice of mercy.

The voice of mercy is also echoed in the lives of three Irish women, ordinary in extraordinary ways. Catherine McAuley, Nano Nagle and Mary Aikenhead are now recognised as women who worked tirelessly to set free the oppressed people of their time. These were women who had great opportunities, but instead they chose shepherding. They were drawn into the heart of mercy, ever radical, always prophetic. In a short space of time they set up a network of schools and hospitals that continue to serve the cause of justice with mercy all over the world. Catherine McAuley, Nano Nagle and Mary Aikenhead are all part of the emergence of the contemporary Irish nation, in the story of education, in the care of the sick, in the freedom of the people. The words of Catherine McAuley reflect the size of mercy: 'We can never say "it is enough".' Mercy is the shepherd's staff.

❧

WHO DO YOU SAY I AM?
Matthew 16:15

It is commonly accepted that the breakdown of trust signals the end of a relationship. When the fracture happens we are left with the question of why we hadn't seen the 'real' person before now? How could we have been so blind. How did we misjudge so badly? Trusting someone deeply means believing that they are who they say they are. It develops when actions and words match and when promises stand the test of time. 'Who do you say that I am?' It is the critical question in every relationship, at every level of society. It governs political decisions and ignites the global markets. It is the challenge in every job interview and the issue in every marriage vow.

Knowing who someone is and loving the discovery is the beginning of trust. We encounter managers and trustees all the time in the commercial world. Somehow we accept that managers have a job to do, but trustees have a word to keep. The concept of trusteeship has taken on a new urgency in our time as we continue to defile the earth and break the sacred trust. Jesus' question about his own identity is inseparable from the question of our own identity. Who do we say that we are?

Jesus is talking covenant here. He has come for the long haul and there can be no misconceptions. His identity, rooted in the village, is already having a global impact. He who walks by the lakeside directs the ocean wave. His Jewish lineage has the DNA of stardust and sunrise, of the first light and of the great *I Am*. He is the trustee of a divine revelation, the link in the chain of creation's destiny. The question is not a theological one; it is a spiritual awakening, a cosmic enlightenment. Like all people entering a life relationship, the disciples have to speak the words of trust, as they have eyes that have seen him and hearts that have loved him. Their future together will depend on this question.

WHERE ARE THE OTHER NINE?
Luke 17:17

Where are the other nine? The perfect number may be ten but it takes the other nine to bring completion. Completion takes everyone. While the question says something about the extent of ingratitude – where is the majority? – it also speaks of the minority and how one single person can change the outcome. One out of ten is small but effective. The one who came back diverts our attention from leprosy to thanksgiving. So the story is really about giving thanks.

What is it about thanksgiving? It establishes a connection between the giver and the receiver. It is a moment of acknowledgement between two people. The other nine, it seems, forgot about the connection. They were happy with physical healing, but that was just the invitation. Jesus was looking for a lifelong conversation. He wanted the ten people on his team. Where had they gone?

There is another aspect to this moving story and it is the issue of remembering. Remembering is the soul of thanksgiving. Jesus promised the totality of his presence in the meal where people gather to remember.

What happens to us when we stop remembering is fragmentation. When birthdays, anniversaries, significant occasions are deleted from our 'to-do' list, the relationship is in trouble. Forgetting is the beginning of frayed edges and we hate ourselves when we forget because everyone is diminished in the process. Today our failure to remember brings tears to the earth and to every living being. The one who came back to give thanks brings us back to remembering.

We talk frequently in life about *finding closure* – that moment when things come together and we are released from unknowing. In the story of the ten lepers we are reminded how remembering to give thanks brings the story to completion. Thanksgiving is about remembering to return, to reconnect, to practice the art of valuing and revering. When we say thanks we acknowledge the source of the blessing and secure the link. One leper returned. He saved the story from going flat. Somehow we remember his return more than his leprosy and we continue to search for the other nine. Mercy is ever grateful.

WOULD YOU BETRAY ME
WITH A KISS?
Luke 22:48

This question sticks in our throats. The deceit that frequently goes with betrayal is the deepest hurt. Betrayal contains falseness when all the little beliefs that we held dearly dissipate. It's the kiss that amplifies this moment of betrayal; when friendship is reduced to mockery. Judas' kiss is a lie. Why did he do it? He knew it was a shameful action and he went as far as he could to cover it up. Judas betrayed himself. Why do we do it?

Judas called the enemies of Jesus to witness the great let down in Christian history. Betrayal is intensified when it goes public and everyone loses. The Judas story sheds a sombre light on our vulnerability when the lure of the profit dulls the mind and the shining silver dazzles our vision. Judas didn't hate Jesus but he saw in the death sentence something for himself. His betrayal with a kiss has turned him into one of the great lepers of biblical history. Part of this isolation is also due to the reality that Judas holds a mirror for us all.

The Gospel mentions the silver – all thirty pieces. Something doesn't add up when we consider how the balance is tipped here. Friendship, promise, commitment and trust are compromised in this moment of madness. Judas got himself entangled in the blur of public opinion, in a value system that destroyed the innocent and called it human rights. The popular voice did his thinking for him and he betrayed his own heart. Judas forgot to stand back and, sadly, his kiss has isolated him from our mercy ever since. As the Jubilee Year of Mercy approaches, however, we have a special opportunity to forgive the Judas kiss.

WHAT DO YOU WANT ME
TO DO FOR YOU?
Mark 10:51

No one can tell us what we want. People make decisions for others all the time, though it rarely works because a decision needs ownership if it is to become an action. At first the question from Jesus to the blind man may sound unnecessary but it is a vital step in the overall story because faith is about decisions and it requires a voice. Faith always speaks, in the silence, in the noise, in the light and in the darkness. Jesus seems to be looking for the kind of faith that speaks out, even when the majority voice finds it embarrassing. In this situation the people scolded the blind man for speaking up!

With the help of modern scholarship we have grown in our understanding of the wisdom and importance of naming what is going on for us. We are repeatedly advised to talk about things and to name our fears and hopes. The story of the blind man invites us to ponder the relationship between physical needs and spiritual needs. It is an insight into the healing of the whole person and helps us to understand how our physical senses channel our deepest needs.

We cannot assume that every blind person is asking for the gift of physical sight. The blind man reminds us that sometimes in life when we get what we want we may find out that it's not what we wanted. So this blind man had to decide. The gift of our senses must never be limited to mere physical dimensions. They take us beyond the known, into the invisible, to the deep waters. They are avenues to the divine encounter, as the blind man discovered. The story takes us into the heart of things.

WHO WILL ROLL AWAY THE STONE FOR US?
Mark 16:3

Stones and buildings go together. When the roof gives way and the plaster crumbles, the stones remain, standing the test of time. In a mysterious way they contain faith, footprints and heartstrings. Stones can be hard as nails or as reliable as a trusted friend. It is really how we perceive them. The stone at the entrance to the tomb on Easter Sunday morning was a force to be reckoned with. It was blocking the entrance, closing off the meeting place. When the women came to perform their ritual of mercy they were faced with the cold, harsh resistance of a blockade. But stones have always given way to mercy and rolled away.

This particular stone, like so many others, was separating friends, closing off the line of communication. The movement of the stone would have to come from within the tomb. An interior strength was required to make the first move. It had been put there by broken relationships, obscene violence and the power of fear. There is no outside power that can remove the stones of our broken relationships. They become lighter, however, when mercy flows into the concrete.

It was the mercy of God that unblocked the entrance to the tomb on Easter Sunday morning. The miracle of kindness softened the burial place and the earth trembled with hope. The stone gave way to mercy on that first Easter day. It is the breakthrough moment for all creation. Where mercy lives, the stone is rolled away.

At the tomb of rebirth we see that within life's most intractable shadows there is a moving light, a rolling stone, a resurrection day.

WOMAN, WHY ARE YOU WEEPING?
John 20:15

The graveyard is frequently the place where the deepest conversations happen. These heart to hearts are mostly spoken in tears when words tend to fail us. Jesus was moved by human tears and he could interpret the script whispered in sorrow. In the garden of the Resurrection, when he met the grieving woman, Jesus broke through her devastation by simply calling her name: 'Mary.' In that single word, the connection was re-established and the veil was pulled back.

He knew her and he called out her name. It was the voice of mercy; he had remembered her and she would remain part of his story beyond the tomb.

There's an awakening in a name. We live in a time of brand names, designer names and domain names. Getting the name right will determine how you proceed in business; dropping the right name in the right places can turn your world around. And so it is that people try to make a name for themselves. What's in a name?

In the garden, when Jesus meets Mary Magdalene, we get another insight into the importance of names. Mary is bewildered as she seeks to bridge the gap between life and death. She helps us to understand the importance of finding the body and the abyss people confront when the body of a loved one is not returned to them. We need a body in order to grieve, to see, to take us through death. Mary Magdalene, like ourselves, is searching for a reference point. Then she hears her name.

He has returned! The body was indeed important. The one who has passed through death still remembers her name, still reaches out in mercy to those who weep. When she heard her name that Easter Sunday morning Mary understood that death itself cannot sever the bonds of affection and that our names are written in the heart of God. When he said her name, she recognised him.

WHAT ARE YOU TALKING ABOUT AS YOU WALK ALONG?
Luke 24:17

What do people talk about after a death? They talk about the one who has died. It is good to talk. Things become clearer, events become purposeful and questions get resolved. Talking is particularly helpful in times of trauma and uncertainty. On the road to Emmaus the two disciples are talking. They are leaving Jerusalem – the scene of darkness – and turning their backs on sorrow. But no one flees from the memory and no one escapes the story. They were struggling and they desperately needed to make sense of the violent death of a good man. Jesus joined them on their route, walking beside them.

The conversation on the road was topical. Jesus helped them to remember. He unravelled the pieces and explained how the whole picture was coming together right before their eyes. The road to Emmaus became for the disciples a time to reconnect the threads and to see the light in the weight of a cross. It was a journey of discovery, an unfolding of the whole picture. For all of us it is an insight into the road of grief, the running away and the slowing down, the listening and the hearing, the companions and the visitor, the silence and the awakening.

One important understanding gleaned on the road to Emmaus is that it was leading somewhere. Although the two mourners did not recognise the Light breaking through, he was there, leading to a new beginning. It was in their loss and confusion that their eyes were opened. Many things helped on the road to discovery. Remembering helped, as did storytelling and family history, but the reassuring presence walking beside them rekindled their hope until it became a fire burning within them. When they reached Emmaus they were ready to revisit the Passover meal.

DO YOU LOVE ME?
John 21: 17

Peter wept when denial overpowered him. Tears have a way of putting things right. The great emotions of gratitude, disappointment, sorrow and joy are best expressed with tears. The global teardrop unites us in our common outcry against the many denials of mercy and justice. Tears are a unique line of communication, a communal sharing. They worked for Peter, and Jesus felt them in his own heart.

The question from Jesus to Peter reminds me of *Fiddler on the Roof* when Tevye asks Golde, his wife of twenty five years, *do you love me?* Golde, it seems, is at first annoyed at what she hears as an unnecessary question. She has given everything to the relationship, a dutiful, responsible, faithful, generous spouse. But is that love, Golde? In the Gospel story, Jesus, like Tevye, raises the bar. Peter is now the leader of an emerging Christian community and as the little gathering grows and matures, it will stand or fall on love. It was time for a second chance for Peter. This was a question of mercy; it thrives on second chances.

The question is communicating the heart and soul of the Incarnation, for God so loved the world that love became flesh in Christ. It was love that took Jesus through the darkest hours of his life. He was misunderstood, misrepresented, misjudged. People all over the world still walk the Stations of the Cross – the graphic reminder of how far love can go. This simple symbolic journey is every human journey. Everyone has somewhere, sometime, held on for love. Tevye was right: love is more that executing a role with great perfection. Love the role.